Hello, Daddy
A Discussion of Christian Prayer

Richard A. Honeycutt, PhD

with
Betty Jane Honeycutt

Illustrations by Chip Holton

Parson's Porch

Parson's Porch Books

Hello, Daddy: A Discussion of Christian Prayer

Copyright © 2012 by Richard A. and Betty Jane Honeycutt

ISBN: 978-1-936912-42-1   **Softcover**

This book was printed in the United States of America.

To order additional copies of this book, contact:

Parson's Porch & Company
1-423-475-7308
www.parsonsporchbooks.com

Acknowledgments

The spiritual influences that brought me to the writing of this book have been many. Starting of course with my parents, Edith and Lester Honeycutt, my guides along the path include Sunday school teachers Maureen Wall, Martha Best, Louise Colvin, and Alvin Philpott; professors Dr. Phyllis Trible, Dr. Robert Helm, and Dr. Kevin Sharpe; and good friend the Rev. Parker McLendon, as well as pastors Dr. J. Roy Clifford, Dr. David Hoke Coon, and Dr. Ray N. Howell III. To these and the countless other fellow seekers, I express deep gratitude.

— Richard A. Honeycutt

I long ago forgot her name. For years I remembered her primarily for her elaborate hats. Yet when various forces tried to drive me from God, her kind words, compassion, and encouragement formed an unbreakable thread— at times, the only thread— that kept drawing me back. She, above all others, is responsible for my loving God and His Word.

Many teachers and friends have influenced my Christian growth, most notably:

Helen McDade Linder, my mentor, encourager, surrogate mother, and friend; Dr. Edgar Christman, who introduced me to the writings of Frederick Buechner; The Rev. Parker McLendon, long-time Sunday school teacher; Dr. David Hoke Coon, who brought Scripture to life with "holy imagination"; Dr. J. Christian Wilson, professor of religion and New Testament Greek; Dr. Ray N. Howell III, Bible study leader extraordinaire.

But I wouldn't have met these wonderful people were it not for the lady with the fancy hats. She taught the fourth-grade girls' Sunday school class in the church where I grew up. To her I offer my deepest thanks for transforming my life, by bringing me to the Light.

— Betty Jane Honeycutt

Table of Contents

Introduction

Do you pray? A recent poll[1] asked this question of a broad sampling of Americans. Most (some 78%) answered "yes". These included both those who attend some form of worship service regularly and those who do not.

Are your prayers answered? Again, the poll revealed that most people who pray do find that at least some of their prayers are answered.

When we look at the usual gauges of our culture— TV, movies, newspapers, and magazines— we would hardly expect these findings. The secular influences that surround us seem much more the norm than does the head bowed in prayer. Certainly devotees of practically all major religions are encouraged to pray. But finding that large numbers of people actually do so is both surprising and comforting.

Are you comfortable with the way you pray? The Gallup poll did not address this question. Many people feel inadequate in their efforts to communicate with God. For some, this inadequacy has led them to abandon the practice entirely. Others persist, knowing all the while that their prayer life could be much better. If you are in either of these groups, this book is addressed to you. I certainly do not know all the answers to an effective prayer life, and make no pretense to even be an expert in the field. But I have sought for years to better understand prayer, to raise my prayers above the common, everyday levels. In this book I will share some things I have learned, and perhaps one or two of these will resonate within you and aid you in your search. If so, I will have succeeded.

---

[1]Kenneth Woodward, et al, "Talking to God," *Newsweek* (Jan. 6, 1992): 38-44. See also Andrew Greeley, "Keeping the Faith: Americans Hold Fast to the Rock of Ages," *Omni* 13 (August 1991):11.

I must state clearly at the outset that this book is written from a Christian perspective, because I can write from no other. I am convinced that Jesus of Nazareth has revealed God in His person as fully as humankind can comprehend. Thus, in a special way that no other human can claim, He is the Son of God. In the writings of His friends, we can find clues that will lead us to a fuller understanding of prayer, and to a greater ability to commune with our Creator, who desires our communion much more than we can ever realize.

As a result of the Christian perspective, much of this book will concentrate on the model prayer that Jesus gave us:

> Our Father in heaven,
> Hallowed be thy name.
> Thy will be done, as in heaven so on earth.
> Give us bread for our needs from day to day.
> And forgive us our offenses, as we have forgiven our
>   offenders.
> And do not let us enter into temptation, but deliver us
>   from evil.
> (Matthew 6:9-13a, Lamsa; see also the parallel passage
> in Luke 11:2-4.)

After many years' study, I have come to believe that Jesus gave us this prayer as a framework for our prayers. By understanding it, we come to understand much of His teaching, not only on prayer, but on the Christian life in general. By using this framework intelligently (loving God with our minds), we learn how to pray effectively. This prayer was never meant to be a ritual formula, recited mindlessly as we daydream about other concerns. To do so is as disrespectful to God as to consistently look away from another human who is talking to us. We will carefully examine what Jesus's words in this prayer meant to Him and to the disciples to whom He gave the prayer. In the process, we will hope to discover more clearly what they should mean to us. After studying the model prayer, we will examine other questions concerning the practice of prayer.

A number of times in this book, I will mention specific words used in the Bible. Some of these will be Hebrew words, some Greek, and some Aramaic. Most of the Old Testament, of course, was written in Hebrew. The New Testament was written for the most part in Greek, although some scholars believe that one or more of the books were translated into Greek from Aramaic. At least our oldest manuscripts have a Greek heritage. In the Middle East of Jesus's time, the common language was Aramaic. All good Jews learned Hebrew in the synagogue schools, and they used that language in worship, and perhaps among themselves. Few of the Romans who controlled Palestine made any effort to learn Aramaic; fewer still studied Hebrew. But neither did they impose Latin on their subjects. Instead, they used Greek as the more-or-less common language of the empire. The Greek culture had so dominated the area the Romans conquered that they found it easier to adopt that language than to try to promulgate their own. We know, therefore, that Jesus spoke Hebrew. Because of the time and place in which He lived, and also because of linguistic clues that show through the Greek of the Gospels, we know that He usually taught in Aramaic. He may also have spoken Greek, although this is only conjecture. It seems to me that there is great value in studying some of the specific words used in the Bible, in order to better understand what they meant to the writers. At the same time, I try hard to avoid the questionable practice of attaching great significance to the subtle meanings of words from translations, whether into Latin, English, or any other language.

Now a word about the Bible passages included in this book. To save you the frustration of balancing a Bible upon your lap while you read this book, I have included most of the quotations to which I refer. I have no favorite translation; each has passages in which it seems to me to excel. Therefore I have quoted from several translations. At the end of each Biblical quotation, I have indicated the translation used. The key to the abbreviations follows:

JB .... The Jerusalem Bible
KJV ... . The King James Version
NKJV .... The New King James Version
Lamsa .... Holy Bible from the Ancient Eastern
                                          Texts   (Trans. by George Lamsa)

NASB .... The New American Standard Bible
NEB .... The New English Bible
Rhm .... Rotherham's Emphasized Bible

Finally, about the stories I've used as illustrations. All of these are real, but the names and identifying circumstances have been changed so that my friends will not recognize *their* friends and create embarrassment for all of us!

What is Prayer?

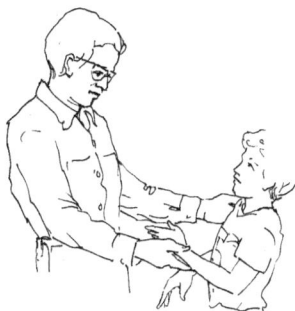

Many practices are called by the name of prayer. Katy kneels beside her bed before going to sleep to recite words she has been taught. Ahmed stands facing east at certain times during the day to utter a ritual formula. Pastor Leonard leads his congregation on Sunday morning. Jerry repeats a memorized blessing before he eats. J. D. bows to open the civic club meeting. The Pharisee stands in the temple while the poor sinner falls to the ground and beats his breast.

What common vein runs through all these examples? In each case, the existence and sovereignty of God are being acknowledged. This alone is a worthy aim. But singing hymns, attending worship services, and even "seeing the sunset and knowing Whom to thank" also acknowledge the existence and sovereignty of God. Prayer can and should be much more. Christian prayer is first and foremost relationship with God. The kind of relationship we will have depends upon our image of God.

One of the most shocking things Jesus did in His earthly ministry was to call God *our Daddy*. The Jewish leaders thought it was so shocking that they called it blasphemy. In fact, the Greek of Mark 14:36 makes no mystery of what word Jesus used to address God; the word *Abba* is simply imported directly from the Aramaic, although the Greek *Pater* is added parenthetically! But the translators of almost all English Bibles think it so shocking that they do not translate the clear Aramaic word *Abba* as *Daddy*, but import it as did the Greek. *Abba* shares its roots with our words *Daddy* and *Mama*: all are copied from babies' early attempts at language. What image does *Daddy* bring to mind? For me it is an adult male on his knees playing with his child. There is strength and protectiveness, but above all there is love and tenderness. The true Daddy is much more than a father. He wants love and fellowship with his children. And as the children grow, he wants to share his knowledge and wisdom about life.

If God is really our Daddy, then how do we relate to Him? First, prayer becomes an act of love, not of obedience or fear or need. It actually becomes a form of visiting, just as we would do with other loved ones. Notice the clear contrast between prayer as visiting and the common misconception of prayer as asking something of God. This misconception leads to much confusion about prayer.

Jamie responded to a knock at the door.

"Ann! I haven't seen you for years! Come in. How are you doing? I've missed you so much!"

"I've missed you, too, Jamie. I was in town and just had to drop by to see you."

How will this story go on? Will Ann sit down by the fire and list half a dozen things that she wants from Jamie? Will she make a memorized speech? Or will she spend her time with her friend by tuning in to Jamie, each sharing with the other? The answer, of course, is clear. If we relate to God in love, then prayer is most importantly attunement with Him.

At some point, Ann may have some favor that she wants to ask of Jamie. Based on their old friendship and their more recent "tuning in" to each other, such a request may be made with perfect naturalness. But the request is not the substance of their reunion; it is only a tangential element.

So part of the confusion about prayer is a language problem. In English, we use the verb *pray*, which has the alternate meaning of *ask*. In Aramaic, the word for prayer is *slotha*, from the root *sla*, meaning "to set a trap". In modern Syriac, which is related to the Aramaic language that Jesus spoke, the word for tuning a radio or television to a particular station comes from the same root. So you trap the signal from the station, or you trap the thoughts of God. Perhaps our first step toward a greater prayer life, then, is to move our focus from asking, to tuning in to God. When we visit or converse with a friend, much of what happens is really driven by the need to tune in with that person. Only when we have really tuned in with each other can we thoroughly enjoy the time together.

How is Prayer Possible?

How can a finite human attune to the infinite Creator? Were we left on our own, it would be a hopeless task. The immense variety of religions that exist and have existed throughout history attest to the efforts of humankind to succeed in that task. Most primitive religions involve some sort of sacrifice. While it can be argued that the sacrifice could have been intended to placate or somehow pay off the god, the practice still involves surrendering something of value. The sacrificial animal was always required to be among the best of the herd or flock. In the "dark religions" (I use the term to describe spiritual darkness) in which human sacrifice was practiced, the victim was most often a young virgin, either male or female. In all cases, the worshipper or worshipping group is giving up something of value in order to at least communicate with the creator. The ancient Hebrews had a very involved and specific set of rules regarding sacrifice. However, their understanding of God grew until the prophet Hosea would say for Him, "I desired mercy, not sacrifice" (Hosea 6:6a, Lamsa). But is not mercy itself a form of sacrifice? When we show mercy toward those who have injured us, are we not sacrificing our feelings of vengeance or self-righteousness or at least injured dignity? These are feelings that seem to have an emotional reward for us, since we do not give them up easily. When we show mercy to one who is financially in our debt, we may be sacrificing material goods just as surely as if we sacrificed an animal from our flock. So one way in which we can attune to God is to habitually show mercy.

Do you notice what we've just said? One of the foremost characteristics of God is His mercy. In order to attune to God, we must habitually show mercy, which makes us more Godlike. Perhaps here is a key to attunement. I am from the South. In my neighborhood, standard English was spoken with a southern accent that had its own local flavor. When I was in high school, I became interested in being a radio announcer. With the help of several good friends, I developed an appropriate "radio voice". With it I worked toward a more neutral accent. When I entered college, I made friendships with people from all across the nation, and my speech changed some more. But even today, when I talk to my family or the friends of my youth, I lapse into something of the old southern accent. I attune with them by behaving more like they do.

Can we attune more easily with God by behaving more like He does? In Leviticus, God repeatedly says to His people, "You shall be holy, for I am holy." But what is it to be holy? Too often we confuse holiness with being holier-than-thou. *Kadish* is the Aramaic word translated *holy.* It means "set apart for a specific purpose." If I have a favorite drinking glass that my family understands is set apart for me, that glass is holy. God, then, is set apart for a particular purpose. He is different; He is other than we are, and there are reason and purpose behind His difference. We are to be set apart for a purpose, and Jesus has revealed what that purpose is: to reconcile God's family to Himself. So being holy doesn't just mean being good; it means being good for something.

Our ideas of holiness are often vague, and they may include things like not drinking alcohol or not smoking, or not eating meat, or not playing cards on Sunday, or even not having fun. When we apply the test of purpose, holiness assumes a much more definite form. Paul says that if my eating meat will weaken a brother in Christ, I should not eat meat. Otherwise, there is no problem with eating meat. Purpose. Too many people who shy away from religion do so because they perceive it to be a system of rules without meaning. The concept of purpose supplies the meaning.

If we focus our whole lives toward bringing ourselves and those we meet closer to Jesus, then holiness follows naturally. How do we do this? Jesus said that whatever we do to the least of His brothers (any member of the human family) we do to Him. As we become more outward-focused, both we and those we help are drawn closer to the Lord.

On one occasion a lawyer came forward to put this test question to him: "Master, what must I do to inherit eternal life?" Jesus said, "What is written in the Law? What is your reading of it?" He replied, "Love the Lord with all your heart, with all your soul, with all your strength, and with all your mind; and your neighbor as yourself." "That is the right answer," said Jesus; "do that and you will live."

But he wanted to vindicate himself, so he said to Jesus, "And who is my neighbor?" Jesus replied, "A man was on his way from Jerusalem down to Jericho when he fell in with robbers, who stripped him, beat him, and went off leaving him half dead. It so happened that a priest was going down by the same road; but when he saw him, he went past on the other side. So too a Levite came to the place, and when he saw him went past on the other side. But a Samaritan who was making the journey came upon him, and when he saw him he was moved to pity. He went up and bandaged his wounds, bathing them with oil and wine. Then he lifted him to his own beast, brought him to an inn, and looked after him there. Next day he produced two silver pieces and gave them to the innkeeper, and said, 'Look after him; and if you spend any more, I will repay you on my way back.' Which of these three do you think was neighbor to the man who fell into the hands of robbers?" He answered, "The one who showed him kindness." Jesus said, "Go and do as he did."
Luke 10:25-37 (NEB)

The Samaritan was outward-focused: he could feel the needs of the victim. The priest and the Levite considered themselves too holy to touch a bloody victim. They were dead wrong. Holiness in this case consisted in following the commandment to love your neighbor as yourself, not the much lesser rule about maintaining ritual purity by not touching blood.

So holiness is not about rules. Jesus lived a life focused on helping others. The sincere intention to follow Him will lead us to holiness.

In my best moments, I approach the level of commitment to Christ that I ought to have. Much of the time, though, I am mired in the concerns of conflicts, schedules, and material things. At these times I often am not very holy. Yet it may be that these are the times when I need prayer most. Not too many people consider the story of Jonah and the whale to be literal history. But it is profoundly true, in the same way that Jesus's parables are true. In a nutshell, Jonah was a preacher. God called him to go to Ninevah to preach repentance to the citizens there. Ninevah was the capital city of the enemy who had been persecuting Jonah's people. Jonah felt very much like the Atlanta Braves' coach would feel if God called him to help the Philadelphia Phillies' star pitcher improve his fast ball. So Jonah ran from God. Hopped a ship heading the other way. When the storm came along and Jonah told the sailors to pitch him overboard, he was not exactly the picture of holiness. (At least he showed the decency to offer his life to save the sailors.) Well, you know the story: the big fish swallowed him up and then Jonah repented and the fish tossed his cookies (or at least his preacher). Then Jonah went and preached a bang-up revival. In fact, the revival was so good that all the Ninevites repented. Jonah was still not very holy. He was mainly hoping to stay around while God blasted Ninevah for her sins. He was seriously disgruntled when they repented and God cancelled the show. But still God was able to speak to him and teach him, even in what were perhaps his unholiest moments. He can do the same for us. Jonah was able to pray when (1) he stopped running from God, and (2) he repented of the major sin that held him. We seldom run from God in such a dramatic way, but when we let other concerns drive God from His proper preeminence in our lives, we are running from Him. So attuning to God when we are not very holy is a two-step process: (1) We must examine ourselves in order to uncover and repent of sins that get in our way, and (2) we must focus on Him. Powerful prayer, then, grows out of a holy life, but God also respects the sincere intention of the moment. It is our individual responsibility to prepare for prayer both through the attunement of our lives and through the attunement of the moment preceding each separate prayer.

Now that we've put the emphasis on purpose, let's get back to the concept of being set apart. When people look at a Christian, what should they see? I think there are two major characteristics. The first is a life turned outward. One day Jesus was on the way to the house of a leader of the synagogue to heal his daughter. This important man could help Jesus's ministry in many ways. Here was a possible gateway to success. On the road, a woman with a hemorrhage (which made her ritually unclean and therefore not even fit to be in public) came up and touched Jesus's robe, desiring to be healed. Jesus felt the power flow, drawn by the woman's faith. Setting aside for the moment the important, politically significant goal toward which He was hurrying, He stopped to affirm and bless this woman who by all standards of the time was less than nobody. His life was always turned outward. How many times do we set aside the cares of our lives to meet another's need?

One day a local teacher stopped by the Interstate highway to help a couple of rather grimy-looking motorists whose old car was spewing radiator coolant. Removing the tool box from his car, he carefully released the pressure on the overheated cooling system and then took out the thermostat, which was stuck closed. As he was replacing the thermostat cover and telling the motorists the location of the nearest service station, one of them asked if he was a preacher. They were looking for a reason why his life was turned outward to help them. This is one thing the world should see when it looks at a Christian.

The other major characteristic that should help to set a Christian apart is even rarer: it is joy. Some of us sing "The Joy of the Lord Is My Strength", but how often do we show that joy? On the night before His crucifixion, Jesus held a celebration and conference with His friends. Some of what He said is recorded in John 14-17. You would think that at a time like this, Jesus would be concerned with who would be in charge after He left, what the disciples should do, and many other details. In John 15:11 He gives the purpose of His whole farewell discourse: "I have spoken thus to you that my joy may be in you, and that your joy may be complete." (NEB) If joy was that important to Jesus, it should be important to us also. How do we experience joy? First, we don't keep our eyes on our problems; we keep them on the Solution. This is not easy, especially at first. But as we practice "praying without ceasing", it begins to become more natural. If prayer is attunement, then to pray without ceasing is to remain tuned in to God all the time. We will find ourselves thanking Him, praising Him, chuckling to Him, and asking Him for help almost unconsciously. This is not a one-week project, though; it is a lifetime practice.

Paul gives us some practical advice on joyful living in Philippians 4:8: "And now, my friends, all that is true, all that is noble, all that is just and pure, all that is lovable and gracious, whatever is excellent and admirable— fill all your thoughts with these things." (NEB) What do we concentrate on most of the time? How many of us start each day with the latest bad news from the TV or newspaper? What do we discuss over lunch? Sometime soon, try holding a conversation with a Christian friend in which neither of you makes any negative statements or suppositions about anyone else, and neither of you talks about how awful something or other is. You may be surprised at just how seldom we do fill our thoughts with things that are true, noble, just, pure, lovable, gracious, excellent, and admirable. To the extent that we do succeed, our joy will grow. As our joy grows, and as we turn our lives outward, we become different from others, and that difference will show. We are being set apart.

So we attune to God by becoming more like Him: we show mercy, we focus on others, we repent of sins, we cultivate joy in our lives.

So far, we have concentrated exclusively on individual prayer. Does this mean that there is something wrong with group prayer? Not at all. "Where two or three have met together in my name, I am there among them." (Matthew 18:20, NEB). What could better characterize ideal prayer than to have the Lord in the midst of those who are praying? However, we have all been exposed to group prayer in many less-than-ideal forms. There is the leader who simply mouths church-sounding phrases, with little thought as to their meaning or appropriateness. There is the pastor who uses the prayer as an extra chance at sermonizing. And certainly there are the congregation members who use group prayer time to file their nails or daydream or catch a little shut-eye. Any of these practices can block the effectiveness of the prayer. Do you notice what is missing in each case? Sometimes the church-sounding phrases induce a worshipful attitude in some members of the group (perhaps by Pavlovian conditioning!). The message in the extra sermon may be valuable and needed. Maybe the nails do need filing. But where is the attunement?

There are two excellent ways for group prayer to work. One is the more traditional way in which a leader speaks for the whole group. We usually think of the leader's position in this case as one of great responsibility. But in fact each member of the group shares equal responsibility. As each line is spoken, each member of the group needs to listen to it, silently agreeing if that is appropriate. Sometimes the leader may offer a phrase to which some of the group cannot assent. When this happens, those members will silently offer their disagreement to God. But in either case, each member of the group has the responsibility of making the prayer his or her own. Some Christian traditions have the beautiful custom of each member offering quiet "amens" as seems appropriate.

The other effective method for group prayer is the one in which group members voice their portions of the prayer in turn. In this method also, each group member is responsible for making each other member's prayer his or her own. In no case is group prayer supposed to be a spectator sport!

Regardless of the form of group prayer, it still must be fundamentally an experience of attuning with God, and this attunement must be individual as well as collective. Often a period of silent attunement can be used before the spoken prayers begin. During this time, each member of the group should try to still the voices of the world and everyday affairs and open his or her heart to the voice of God. This is the attunement of the moment that we discussed earlier.

Our question, "What is prayer?", has led us to an understanding that prayer is attunement with God. We have also found some ways in which we can improve our attunement in our lives as a whole and in the specific moments preceding our prayer time. Now we are ready to study some of our Lord's instructions about the act of prayer itself.

To Whom Do You Pray?

Who is God?

The title of this chapter may seem an unnecessary question. The obvious answer is "to God, of course." But just who is your God? The child's answer of an old man with a long white beard is clearly inadequate. Yet attunement presupposes relationship, and to have a relationship with anyone, we must know something about that person. Various Christian groups have dealt with the question in different ways. We have the angry, vindictive God of some sects, the remote God of others, and the sweet, kind God of still others. C. S. Lewis tells of a young lady who came to him at Cambridge University one day to talk about God. She had rejected the anthropomorphic (human-shaped) image of God with which she had grown up. She felt it was too limiting. By the time she had finished "un-limiting" God, she had settled upon a description which Lewis said was indistinguishable from that of a giant tapioca pudding.

One thing upon which the Bible leaves no doubt is that God is best described as a person, not a pudding. This idea is in direct contrast to the Buddhist concept, in which God is not even universally acknowledged. Buddhists who do acknowledge God are very reticent about trying to describe Him. They feel that to do so is to limit God. The Bible presents a progressive revelation of the nature of God, and one element of the Christian faith is that this revelation is true, because it is God's *self*-revelation. We first meet God the Creator in Genesis 1 and 2. Then Adam sins and we see God the Judge. Cain meets this aspect of God soon thereafter, and we can add the word *merciful* as God agrees to protect Cain from human vengeance.

During Israel's slavery in Egypt, a first-hand knowledge of God seems to have been lost. The reason is not hard to find. Virtually all Biblical scholars agree that the earliest **written** forms of any books of the Bible date from well after the deliverance from Egypt. So transmission of stories showing God's self-revelation would have depended upon word of mouth. Recent anthropological studies of numerous primitive tribes have shown that oral history can be preserved with amazing accuracy through many generations, because the ability to memorize and repeat the story of one's ancestors— personal or tribal— was considered essential to acceptance as an adult. However, both the ability and the will to transmit the old lore are needed, and with the descendants of Jacob living in a strange land among worshippers of multiple gods for four hundred years, it is not surprising that the will of the numerous "younger generations" to memorize tribal history would have wavered.

A careful reading of Exodus does not reveal a people who had retained a vital sense of God's presence in their daily lives, but rather a people who had some collective memory of their God, with widely varying degrees of commitment to Him. Much of Moses's work of building the Hebrew nation involved serving as an intermediary for God's re-revelation of Himself. So in Exodus we see God the Deliverer, God the Ruler of the Universe, and God the Maker of History. As the revelation progresses, all the earlier features of God's nature are reinforced, and hints of new themes begin to appear. For example, Dathan and his family challenged Moses's authority and got a personal revelation of God the Judge. (See the fifteenth chapter of Numbers.) And at several points in the elaboration of the Law (such as Exodus 20:6 and Deuteronomy 13:12-18) we begin to see hints of God the Giver of Mercy. By the time we get to the books of the prophets, we have witnessed a growing revelation of God's mercy, like the development of a motif in a mighty symphony, until it commands equal attention with judgment.

In order to understand how far God's self-revelation had been understood by the Jews of Jesus's time, let us look at a few facts. The Holy Name YHWH (shown in most English translations as "the LORD") was first used in Genesis 2:5. Soon thereafter, we are told, "Seth too had a son, whom he named Enosh. At that time men began to invoke the LORD by name." (Genesis 4:25b-26, NEB). When Moses confronted the burning bush (Exodus 3:3 and following), he asked God to reveal His name. Let's examine some reasons that Moses may have asked for God's name, because there is more in this question than meets the eye. First, Moses knew the names of many gods, since he had been raised as an Egyptian prince. Here was a God whose power Moses had actually experienced, a God to whose reality he could attest. Naturally he wanted to know whether this was one of the gods he had heard about, or perhaps an entirely new one. Second, Moses would need to be able to tell the Hebrews just which god he was working for. Perhaps some of them remembered the Name by which their ancestors used to call upon God. Third, Middle-Easterners of Moses's time recognized more clearly than we do that knowing someone's name gives us power over that person. If you and I were at a party, and you wanted to attract my attention from across the room, you would have a much easier time doing so if you knew my name. And in fact I would find it extremely difficult to ignore your calling me by name. The Egyptian priests were considered to have the power of influencing their gods. It is conceivable that Moses had absorbed the desire to manipulate God, which would require knowing His Name. Fourth, there is the possibility that Moses thought God would not give His name, since titles rather than names were used for other Middle-Eastern gods. (*Molech* means *king,* and *Baal* means *lord.*) Then Moses could have used this refusal to bolster his own refusal to go to Egypt as God had commanded. Probably for all these reasons, Moses asked God's name. We still do not absolutely know the answer He gave. Very ancient Hebrew writing only included consonants. We know that the consonants in God's answer transliterate into English as YHWH. Later, vowel points were added to represent vowels. German theologians speculated that the Name would have been pronounced "Ye – ho – wah" which of course would have been spelled "Jehovah" in German. This spelling, but with Anglicized pronunciation, was adopted wholesale in English for many years. Most present-day Hebrew scholars think that a more likely rendering is Yahweh.

Just what does *Yahweh* mean? No one can really give us an absolute answer. Our best guess is that it is related to the Hebrew verb "to be". Thus it can perhaps be translated as "I am who I am" or "I will be what I will be". In the second and third centuries B.C., a group of eminent Hebrew scholars gathered to translate the Hebrew scriptures into Greek, because of the large and growing number of Hebrews who lived in Greek-speaking areas, many of whom could no longer read Hebrew. This translation is called the Septuagint, since legend has it that there were seventy scholars. In the Septuagint, the Name is translated "I am The Being." Just what kind of meaning can we find in these translations? In every case, there is emphasis upon the existence of God. All the other gods could in reality be named "I am not." The translation in the Septuagint goes further. It implies that there is but one living Being, and that Being is God. Before we jump to condemn this idea as pantheism (the identification of the created universe with God), let us remember that Paul implied approval of identifying God as the one in whom "we live and move and have our being." (Acts 17:28). And Paul was on solid theological ground:

> LORD, Thou hast examined me and knowest me.
> Thou knowest all, whether I sit down or rise up;
> > thou hast discerned my thoughts from afar.
> Thou hast traced my journey and my resting places,
> > and art familiar with all my paths.
> For there is not a word on my tongue
> > but thou, LORD, knowest them all.
> Thou hast kept close guard before me and
> > behind and hast spread thy hand over me.
> Such knowledge is beyond my understanding,
> > so high that I cannot reach it.
> Where can I escape from thy spirit?
> > Where can I flee from thy presence?
> If I climb up to heaven, thou art there;
> if I make my bed in Sheol, again I find thee.
> If I take my flight to the frontiers of the morning
> > or dwell at the limit of the Western sea,
> even there thy hand will meet me
> > and thy right hand will hold me fast.
> If I say, "Surely darkness will steal over me,
> > night will close around me",
> darkness is no darkness for thee
> > and night is as luminous as day;
> > to thee both dark and light are one.
> Psalm 139: 1-12 (NEB)

So far, we have a tapestry of a God who really *is*, and whose nature includes creativity, power, justice, and mercy. But there is no thread in this tapestry to indicate that God is approachable. In fact, although God said to Moses, "Yahweh... is my name for all time; by this name shall I be invoked for all generations to come" (from Exodus 3:15, JB), this same God was, by Jesus's time, considered so holy and unapproachable that His Name could not be uttered. This prohibition arose from priests and scribes considering the third commandment: "You shall not take the Name of Yahweh your God in vain." "Taking the name" of a god was frequently done in everyday life, to bolster the credibility of someone's statements. Merchants would frequently swear by the name of their god(s) that a certain item was genuine or valuable or of high quality. Jesus taught against this practice:

> Again, you have learned that our forefathers were told, "Do not break your oath," and, "oaths sworn to the Lord must be kept." But what I tell you is this: You are not to swear at all— not by heaven, for it is God's throne, nor by earth, for it is his footstool, nor by Jerusalem, for it is the city of the great King, nor by your own head, because you cannot turn one hair of it white or black. Plain "Yes" or "No" is all you need to say; anything beyond that comes from the devil.
> Matthew 5:33-37 (NEB)

It seems plain to us that the third commandment was intended not to prohibit the use of the Name, but to prevent its *abuse*. However, legalists decided that forbidding the use of the Name at all was prudent. (It was men of the same school of thought who decided that a walk of a certain distance was permissible on the Sabbath, but one step farther was considered working. Washing dishes was legal, but throwing out the dishwater could accidentally cause a seed to sprout and thereby constitute planting, which was forbidden on the Sabbath.) The force of this prohibition was so strong that even English translations of the Bible have only begun using the name Yahweh within the last two decades or so (in spite of Joseph Bryant Rotherham's clearly reasoned plea in the introduction to his 1902 translation of the Scriptures). Almost all earlier translations (as well as some newer ones) render the Name as "the LORD." From our modern perspective, we may have trouble understanding a concept of a God who is so remote. But the entity we have just described is exactly an idealized benevolent Middle-Eastern king of almost any time before the Christian era. The god of the average Jew in the last century B.C. was just a good earthly king writ large.

Father

Jesus of Nazareth's birth opens an unprecedented chapter in God's self-revelation. For the first time, humankind could directly witness the way God would behave in many common situations. The picture of God that emerged from Jesus's earthly ministry was predominantly one of love and mercy, but love and mercy that expect humanity's response. "Here I stand knocking at the door; if anyone hears my voice and opens the door, I will come in and sit down to supper with him and he with me." (Revelation 3:20, NEB). Throughout the Bible, no characteristic of God that was revealed earlier is negated, but at each step, a fuller picture of His nature emerges. No rational person would expect that finite humans could fully comprehend an infinite God, but Christians believe that God has chosen to reveal all of Himself that finite humans can understand, and that He has done it through Jesus.

It is very important not to think that we ever know enough about God that we have Him in a box. We have an invaluable book. A relatively small portion of that book describes the earthly ministry of Jesus. But all the events described in the Gospels would only take a few months at most. Jesus lived on earth for about thirty-three years. There is very much about His brief ministry that we do not know. There is much more about the Lord Jesus Himself that we do not know. And the distinction between Jesus as the Son of God and God the Father is also crucial, but no human can fully describe that relationship. God is much more than any human can comprehend. Jesus could only show us those elements of God's nature that could be expressed in human form. The main reason that Christians have embraced the concept of the Trinity is that we know that in seeing Jesus we see God (John 14:9), and yet we also know that Jesus is not the Father, since He Himself prayed to the Father on many occasions.

When we pray, do we pray to Jesus, or to God? One day Jesus's disciples asked Him to teach them to pray, just as John the Baptizer taught his disciples to pray. Jesus began by saying "When you pray, say, 'Our Father, Who is in the heavens.' " (Matthew 6:9b, Rhm) As we mentioned earlier, Jesus's word translated *Father* is considered by almost all students of the Bible to have been the Aramaic child's cry, *Abba*. The sense of tenderness and intimate relationship conveyed by His use of this word is inescapable. The shock that this form of address caused the leading Jews has already been discussed. Perhaps they did not notice that even more shockingly, Jesus directed the disciples to pray to "*Our* Daddy". The same God who is Daddy to our Lord Jesus is also Daddy to us. John puts it this way: "Here and now, dear friends, we are God's children; what we shall be has not yet been disclosed, but we know that when it is disclosed we shall be like him, because we shall see him as he is." (1 John 3:2, NEB) You and I are God-class beings. Sheep do not give birth to pigeons, nor can a bull father a rabbit. If God is our Daddy, then we are indeed created in His image and likeness.

What about Jesus being the only-begotten Son of God? Paul tells us that Jesus is "the eldest among a large family of brothers". (Romans 8:29, NEB) We became His siblings through the final act of our creation, which was our personal salvation. We do not crawl as abject slaves into the throne room of an oriental despot to beg a boon; we walk confidently into the presence of the Creator and Sustainer of the Universe to fellowship with Him, because He is Our Daddy!

If you find yourself fearing a lightning bolt as you contemplate this fact, remember that you are in the company of the most religious people of Jesus's time (and many later times, also). But read the words of Scripture:

> But to all who did receive him [Jesus], to those
> who have yielded him their allegiance, he gave
> the right to become children of God, not born of

any human stock, or by the fleshly desire of a
human father, but the offspring of God himself.
(John 1:12-13, NEB)

For all who are moved by the Spirit of God are
sons of God.
(Romans 8:14, NEB)

To prove that you are sons, God has sent into
our hearts the Spirit of his Son, crying 'Abba,
Father!' You are therefore no longer a slave but a
son...
(Galatians 4:6-7a, NEB)

Show yourselves guileless and above reproach,
faultless children of God in a warped and
crooked generation, in which you shine like stars
in a dark world and proffer the word of life.
(Philippians 2:15-16a, NEB)

It is important for us to realize just what our relationship with God is
if we are to pray effectively, because only in understanding our
relationship with God can we know God as Jesus intended. If, then,
God is our Daddy, what does that tell us about Him? First, we can
depend upon Him to meet our needs. It is crucial here to remember
that He "knows what your needs are before you ask him." (Matthew
6:8b, NEB) He also knows the things we desire, and think we need,
but may or may not actually need. A newborn baby knows primarily
pain and pleasure. The infant perceives two needs: to be free from
pain, and to experience pleasure. The baby's parents know other
things that the baby needs— adequate nutrition, exercise, fresh air,
attention— and they provide them. The teenage child may imagine
that (s)he needs a new car, many compact disks, and expensive
clothes. These desires may well be so intense at times that they feel
like needs. But again the parents know the difference between needs
and desires. In fact, good parents often try very hard to give the child
the things (s)he desires but does not need, all the while recognizing
the difference between desires and needs. God does the same.

Second, He cares about us even more deeply than we care about ourselves. We do not need to "go babbling on like the heathen who imagine that the more they say the more likely they are to be heard." (Matthew 6:7, NEB) In other words, we do not need to do something to get God's attention; we already have it. A child will often do cute, irritating, or even dangerous things to get the attention of his or her parents. Unfortunately, these attention-getting maneuvers are often necessary because of the human parents' limited ability to focus on each of the stimuli in their lives. God has no such limitation. When we speak, He hears.

Third, God has emotions. This statement would be considered hopelessly naïve by many of the world's religions. Their argument goes something like this: God is by definition perfect. Perfection means that He is absolutely complete. If He is complete, then He can have no needs. Certain emotions, such as the feeling of rejected love and loneliness, imply a need. Therefore, God cannot have emotions. This argument is not Christian. In fact, emotions are more accurately considered as another kind of sense organ. We sense heat by the specialized nerves in our skin; we sense sound by the specialized nerves in our ears. We sense rejected love and loneliness and joy and peace through our emotions. A god without emotions could not sense these things, and would in fact not be perfect at all. Further, if God had no needs, then why create at all? Even aside from the Christian assertions of God's nature, I think we can state that God has the need to create, and the need for relationship with His creation. In fact, the need for relationship may be the seed of the need to create. If we imagine the ideal human father, we find the need to relate to, and provide for, his family to be one of his foremost attributes. I believe that it is so with God.

A number of years ago, I read of a missionary who visited a rather primitive tribe. He introduced himself and told the chief and the tribal leaders that he was there to teach them about God. Then he began to describe God as a father. Immediately he noticed that his listeners began to appear very frightened and dismayed. After further discussions, he discovered that the image of a father in this tribe was very macho, and not at all caring. When fathers interacted with their families at all, it was in a very rough, superior manner. All concepts of loving, caring, tenderness, and providing for the family were associated with the mother. Tragically, many people in our contemporary society have grown up with a similarly damaged image of "father." If your image of a father is of one who is abusive, dictatorial, or remote and uncaring, then although you can probably imagine an ideal father, you may not find the ability to trust and feel comfortable with anyone called by that title. The subconscious mind is only poorly understood, but we know that impressions made upon it can have profound effects upon our attitudes and emotions. The missionary mentioned above explained to the tribal leaders the difference between their concept of "father" and his own. He then began describing God as an ideal mother. As a result, a great Christian work was started among these people.

Many sincere Christians wonder whether it is right to describe God as Mother, since the image in the New Testament is clearly masculine. They fear that to do so is just another example of letting our society shape our religion. Let us examine this question carefully. First, what is the essence of masculinity and of femininity? The teachers of mythology and literature tell us that the masculine image (the *animus* in the terminology of Carl Jung) includes the elements of provider, protector, dominator, even aggressor. The feminine image (the *anima*) is creative, nurturing, caring, loving, and when considered in relationship to a baby, it is also a provider, specifically of nourishment. At this point it is essential to mention that no real human is exclusively masculine or feminine; all have aspects of both. In fact, psychologists agree that psychological balance requires both. But one or the other is predominant.

What do we know about God? Certainly the terms *male* and *female* do not apply, because these terms refer to physical characteristics. We have all seen examples of very feminine males, and very masculine females, so we distinguish between physical gender and psycho-spiritual gender. The question becomes: Is God masculine or feminine? Let us look first at the names used for God in the Old Testament. We have already examined the Name, Yahweh, which expresses what some have called "is-ness." Sometimes this Name is used in the compound *Yahweh Sabaoth*, meaning "Yahweh of the Hosts," often rendered as the "LORD of Hosts."

In a great many places, God is called *Elohim*, which is actually a plural form meaning simply "gods". The reason for the plural form is thought to be the same as for the "plural of majesty," which historically has been used by kings, as in, "We are pleased to introduce our consort, Lady Elenor," meaning, "Hey folks, meet my wife."

Another word translated as *God* is *El*, which is a very ancient name for God used throughout the Middle East. The word passed into Aramaic as *Al*, and into modern Arabic as *Allah*. Some scholars say that the best translation for *El* is "essence." However that may be, the word can certainly be translated as a generic name for God. You can see the *El* root in all of the common Old Testament names for God, except for the Name He gave Himself: *Yahweh*.

God is sometimes called *Elda'ah*, meaning "god of knowledge".

El Shaddai is the name usually used for God in Genesis, especially in connection with the covenant of Abraham. Again we see the *El* root. Traditionally, *Shaddai* has been translated "Almighty," assuming that *Shaddai* was derived from the root *shadad*, meaning powerful. Most scholars now think that the correct derivation is from *shad*, meaning "breast." This name clearly conveys the concept of God as the provider of sustenance!

El Elyon pertains to God in relation to Jerusalem; its traditional translation of "God Most High" is probably correct.

El Olam is used regarding God at Beer-sheba, and it means "Everlasting God."

El Roi, "God of Seeing," is used to denote God at an unnamed sacred place in the wilderness, and is used in the sense of "God of a vision" in the story of Hagar in Genesis 16.

There is in fact no gender associated with any of these Old Testament names for God, except for *El Shaddai*, which is decidedly feminine. On the other hand, Jesus clearly chose the masculine parent image to represent God. Why is this? Let me offer a theory. Remember Matthew 19:2-6:

> Some Pharisees came and tested him by asking, "Is it lawful for a man to divorce his wife on any and every ground?" He asked them in return, "Have you never read that the Creator made them from the beginning male and female?"; and he added, "For this reason a man shall leave his father and mother, and be made one with his wife; and the two shall become one flesh. It follows that they are no longer two individuals: they are one flesh. What God has joined together, man must not separate.
> (NEB)

Alongside this passage, remember that Adam was the original Man, and that Eve (Woman) was taken from him. Both the Matthew and the Genesis passages imply that God's plan for humans involved a union of male and female principles. Notice that Eve was not created separately; she was created *from Adam.* Adam (God's prototype human) originally was *male and female.* Not either-or, but both-and! (Whether you take the first chapters of Genesis literally or symbolically makes no difference here, the point is the same.) What does Jesus say? "...the Creator made them from the beginning male and female..." Not *male or female.* Only if we notice the *and* does the rest of the passage from Matthew make sense: "... a man shall be *made one* with his wife, and the two shall become *one flesh.*" [Emphasis added.] A man and a wife truly (not symbolically) become united through what Dr. D. Hoke Coon called "that marvelous divine arithmetic in which one plus one equals one!" If Christian men and women realized the depth of union that marriage represents, there might be fewer marriages, but there would certainly be fewer divorces. Most of this irrelevant stuff about individuals not being fulfilled in a marriage would fall by the wayside, because "they are no longer two individuals: they are one flesh."

Have I digressed? Not at all. If humans were made in God's image, and He made them from the beginning male *and* female, then God is

Himself masculine and feminine. So the answer to our question, "Is God masculine or feminine?" is "No." Did Jesus teach this? Not directly, although, as you can see, He gave us the key. Our society may well not be ready for the concept that gender is a human limitation that simply does not apply to God. And if our society is not ready for this idea, certainly the society in first-century Palestine was not. At that time, a common prayer among Jewish men was, "Thank you, O Creator of the Universe, for not making me either a slave, a Gentile, or a woman." Men would not speak to any woman in public, even their wives. Women were relegated to an inferior section of the temple during worship. Even the apostle Paul showed definite sexist bias in some of his writings. Educators know that the first job of any teacher is to create learning readiness. The people of Jesus's day certainly were not ready to learn that God might be anything more than strictly masculine. But Jesus planted the seeds to change that. He spoke to the woman at the well in Samaria, even though she was a woman *and* a Samaritan. Notice the amazement with which John reports: "At that moment his disciples returned and were astonished to find him talking with a woman; but none of them said, 'What do you want?' or 'Why are you talking with her?' " (John 4:27, NEB) The first few verses of Luke 8 tell us that a group of women traveled with Jesus, providing for his ministry out of their own resources. According to Luke, the resurrected Jesus appeared first to women, then later to his male disciples. In Romans 16:1, Paul says: "I commend to you Phoebe, a fellow-Christian who holds office in the congregation at Cenchrae." (NEB) The Greek is less mealy-mouthed than most of our translations. The words translated, "who holds office in the congregation," are *ousan diakonon tē ekklēsias*, "being a deacon of the church". Everywhere male deacons are mentioned in the New Testament, the word used is *diakonos*, the nominative form of *diakonon*, which is in the accusative case. Yet most translators shy away from admitting that Phoebe was a deacon. Need I say more about the readiness of our own society to accord women the status that Jesus intended? And only when we are able to fully understand that the feminine and the masculine principles are equally valuable in God's sight, will we truly be able to handle the gender-inclusiveness of God Himself.

Today humans are either male or female, so Jesus could not create a useful parallel in his hearers' minds by calling God his "Father-Mother" or "Daddy-Mama." Therefore, He used the masculine image, although I am convinced that His understanding included both genders. As Jesus accepted our human limitations by referring to God as his Father or Daddy, so shall I.

All this brings up what is perhaps a trivial question: What about the pronoun? Unfortunately, we do not have a gender-inclusive pronoun in English. Centuries of tradition have taught the use of *he, him, and his* when gender could not be specified. There are four other alternatives. We can stick with nouns and avoid the use of pronouns entirely (awkward); we can use *it* (but *it* is gender-*ex*clusive, not inclusive, and implies non-personhood); we can always say *he or she, him or her, his or hers* (wordy); or we can invent new pronouns (probably the ultimate solution, but not within my purview as an individual author). Therefore, I have chosen to continue the tradition followed by English writers throughout history and use the masculine pronoun to represent uncertain or inclusive gender, relying upon my readers to have the open-mindedness to understand what is meant. I believe you are up to the task. What you do in your own writing is up to you!

Our Father

We have already noticed that Jesus said to pray to *our* Father, which means that the Father of Jesus is the Father of us also: not just Jesus's Father and my Father and your Father, but the Father of every human being. This was an idea that Jesus's fellow Jews found hard to stomach. From the time of Abraham forward, the Hebrews were taught that God had a special relationship with the Jews, that He had chosen them. They were to be different from the neighboring tribes. Gradually, God revealed that He had chosen this people for no less purpose than the redemption of humankind. The story of the Hebrews until about 587 BC was one of wandering from God in an effort to be more like their neighbors, including worshipping other gods. Periodically a calamity would befall them, or a great prophet would arise (often both) and the people would return to God for a short time before wandering again. But in 587 BC, Jerusalem fell to the Babylonians under Nebuchadnezzar, which began the period of the Babylonian exile. After returning from the exile, the Jews (for the other tribes were lost, leaving only Judah) never again participated in idol worship. The lesson of their peculiar relationship with God had sunk in. But if you read Nehemiah, you will find that an intense nationalism grew up at the same time. It was a nationalism that said not only, "We are different, because we are chosen," but also, "We are better because we are chosen." They had lost sight of the distinction between being chosen for mission and being chosen for privilege.

The book of Acts is filled with examples of the Jews having trouble accepting Gentiles as persons, much less equals. After the church at Jerusalem finally admitted that God would save Gentiles (Acts 11:18), many Jewish Christians still maintained for years that a person had to become fully Jewish, be circumcised, and keep the Law, before (s)he could become a Christian. (See, for example, Galatians 1:1 through 5:12.)

What does this have to do with us? It means that each human being is our brother or sister, because we all have the same Father. There is therefore no ground for a Christian to discriminate against others on basis of race, gender, political persuasion, or any other superficial grouping. We implicitly recognize this fact when we pray to Our Father.

In the Heavens

The word *heaven* or *the heavens* in English can mean either the physical universe that seems to be "above" the earth, or the spiritual abode of God. The Hebrew *samayim* and the Greek *ouranos* (and its plural, *ouranoi*) carry exactly the same literal meanings. So Jesus could be just indicating God's address when He instructs us to pray to *Our Daddy in the heavens*. If our prayers were carried by some sort of divine postal service, this might make sense. But I believe that Jesus's meaning is more important than this. Besides the literal meanings, the Hebrew, English, and Greek words for *heaven* also have a symbolic meaning. As the place where God lives, heaven is the controlling part of the cosmos, which consists of heaven and earth. Baseball fans may say that Atlanta has defeated Philadelphia, when they mean that a team called the Atlanta Braves has defeated a team called the Philadelphia

Phillies. In the same way, God's action in relation to earth— the Creator's action in relation to the creation— can be referred to by using the words *heaven* and *earth*. When Jesus addresses *Our Daddy in the heavens*, He alludes to the divine rulership and awesome power of God. Here He balances the familiarity of *Daddy*. Following His example, we address our prayers to The Being who has an intimate relationship with each of us but who is nevertheless all-powerful and commands the utmost respect! We acknowledge both a profound likeness and an equally profound otherness. The balance is essential for us to properly relate to God. Too much familiarity makes us take Him too lightly. Too much respect makes Him seem too remote to care about us. But as Jesus has taught us, God is Our Daddy in the heavens.

Hallowed Be Your Name

The word *hallow* means "to make holy." We have already looked at the Aramaic root word for *holy* that Jesus probably employed (Chapter 1), and learned that it means "set apart for a specific purpose". But what was Jesus's purpose in including this phrase? Let's take a closer look.

One possibility for Jesus's meaning is that this is just a Middle-Eastern formula for respect. It was (and often still is) common for Middle-Easterners to address their rulers as "King So-and-So, may you live forever." Nobody— including the king himself— expects the king to live forever, and in fact some of his ministers who use this formula may well be plotting that he may die tomorrow. But the phrase is recognized by all as an expression of respect to the ruler. God, on the other hand, will certainly live forever, so a different phrase is called for. We often address God as Creator and Sustainer of the universe. He knows that He is these things; we know that He is these things; and He knows that we know that He is these things! But we say the words anyway to show respect. "Hallowed be Your Name" would fit well into the form used for such expressions.

The problem with this interpretation is that it ignores the fact that Jesus showed no inclination to use purely ceremonial phrases at any other point in his ministry. I think there is more here. A careful comparison of the meaning of this second phrase with the Third Commandment reveals a striking similarity. In order to see this similarity, we first have to strip the commandment of a couple millenias' misinterpretation. The Third Commandment does not prohibit the use of profane language. (There are several passages in the Bible that do, however.) The King James Version renders it "Thou shalt not take the name of the LORD thy God in vain." The English language has changed in the more than four centuries since the KJV was published. The New English Bible better captures the meaning for today's reader: "You shall not make wrong use of the name of the LORD your God." (Exodus 20:7a) If you and I were to go visit Honest Abdul's used camel lot, and we two green foreigners (I don't know the Arabic for *suckers*) asked to look at a low-priced used camel, we would soon begin to hear declarations of the youth and strength and endurance and noble parentage of the flea-bitten bag of bones that was being urged upon us. These declarations would almost certainly be "strengthened" by numerous oaths, sworn on Abdul's ancestors, his wife's honor, his own head, his place of worship, and maybe even his god. It is this practice that the Third Commandment prohibits. (Please understand that I intend no disrespect to Arabian merchants; I simply state a fact of the Middle-Eastern market-place, and of many other market places, for that matter.) Jesus Himself had just addressed this matter shortly before He gave us his model prayer. He said:

> You are not to swear at all— not by heaven, for it is God's throne, nor by earth, for it is his footstool, nor by Jerusalem, for it is the city of the great king, nor by your own head, because you cannot turn one hair of it white or black. Plain "yes" or "no" is all you need to say; anything beyond that comes from the devil. (Matthew 5:34b-37, NEB)

So we are not to swear at all, and certainly not by God's Name. In our time, the phrase, "by God, I'll [do this or that]," is a more contemporary example of what Jesus forbade. We have not used God's Name, but rather His title. To most of us, however, the word *God* means just what *Yahweh* would have meant to a first-century Hebrew. It may be argued that "by God" is not intended as an oath at all. But this is precisely the point. Using the form of an oath without intending the significance of an oath represents thoughtless speech. This is a wrong use of any word that refers to God. So is the use of the word *God* in cursing. James says, "Out of the same mouth come praises and curses. My brothers, this should not be so." (James 3:10, NEB) "Cursing," as used in the Bible, has a very specific meaning. It means to proclaim unfavorable judgment upon someone or something, often invoking God in the process. Not all use of profane language is cursing. Not all cursing involves use of profane language. But whenever we use the word *damn* as an interjection, especially when we insert *God* in front of it, we are cursing. James says all cursing is wrong. Paul says, "Call down blessings on your persecutors— blessings, not curses." (Romans 12:12, NEB) The sign of the Christian is the blessing. Often we curse thoughtlessly, as an expression of anger. Again, we are not to speak thoughtlessly, but "Whoever loves life and would see good days must restrain his tongue from evil..." (1 Peter 3:10, NEB)

What, then, do we accomplish by praying to God that His Name be hallowed? First, we affirm Jesus's teaching about the proper use of the Name. The second phrase in the Lord's Prayer is then not a request, but an affirmation. In saying it, we are not trying to change God's actions (a bit of a silly idea, don't you think?) but to change ourselves. Have you ever taken part in a school pep rally? What is the purpose of the pep rally? Is it to psyche up the team? Well, partly. But the players have been practicing every day, and we would expect that they are already motivated to do their best. At least part of the purpose of the pep rally is to psyche up the supporters of the team. Whether true or not, it is generally believed that the team will be emotionally invigorated by an enthusiastic, cheering crowd. So in the pep rally, the crowd is enjoined to repeat ritual formulas which are intended to excite and motivate the crowd members themselves. The principle is the same as that of reciting the pledge of allegiance to the flag. Again, the intended effect is upon the individual doing the reciting.

Prayer is attunement with God. A very important step is speaking words that promote our thinking in ways that help us attune. As we pray, "Hallowed be Your Name," we do this.

There's more. As God's family, we are known by His Name! If we were to meditate upon this fact until we fully understood it, it would transform everything that we think or do. For many of us, this may be too powerful a concept to really believe. Yet in Chronicles 7:14 God refers to the nation of Israel as "My people who are called by my name". Christians are baptized in the name of the Father, the Son, and the Holy Spirit. In fact, the Greek is more specific. The preposition translated *in* is *eis*, which is more precisely translated *into*. We are baptized *into* the name of the Father, the Son, and the Holy Spirit! "For God so loved the world that he gave his only begotten son, that everyone believing into him should not perish, but have everlasting life." (John 3:16, NKJV) James speaks of the "honored name by which God has claimed you". (James 2:7, NEB)

For many centuries, a son of a noble house wore or carried a signet ring. Whenever he entered into a financial transaction, he would use the signet ring to stamp a hot-wax seal on the documents involved. The seal was a symbol of the family. The transaction was completed in the name of the house, not in the name of the son. It was backed by the honor of the whole noble family, not just the honor of one man.

When I negotiated my first auto loan, I dealt with a lender with whom my father had dealt for many years. I received the loan without the usual hassle that a person with no established credit must endure. The loan was made because of my father's good name. His name represented his character.

Since we are known by God's Name, everything we do reflects upon the character of God. When we are less than Christian, we drag His Name down with us. This is the opposite of hallowing the Name. When we live in a Christlike way, we are hallowing God's Name. So when we pray "hallowed be Your Name," we are also affirming our intention to honor God with our lives. Sometimes I become aware of a particular weakness in my Christian walk that does not honor Him. I think it is very appropriate to add specific prayers about this weakness as I pray for God's Name to be hallowed. Prayer for God's help in our personal spiritual growth is always blessed, and this point in the Lord's Prayer is an excellent time to make such a request.

Thy Kingdom Come,
Thy Will Be Done,
On Earth As In Heaven

Thy Kingdom, Thy Will

If we were to ask a fifth-grade student, "What is poetry?" we would likely get an answer that involved rhyming words or at least a rhythm. Of course much poetry has neither rhyme nor rhythm, but our most basic conceptions of poetry usually include these elements. Hebrew poetry is very different. The primary distinguishing characteristic of Hebrew poetry is parallelism. This occurs in two forms. One is *synonymous* parallelism, in which the poem is written in couplets; the second line of each couplet says the same thing as the first, but with a slightly different slant. For example:

> O LORD, do not rebuke me in thy anger,
>   nor punish me in thy wrath.
> For thou hast aimed thy arrows at me,
>   and thy hand weighs heavy upon me.
> Thy indignation has left no part of my body
> unscarred;
>   there is no health in my whole frame because of
> my sin.
> (Psalm 38:1-3, NEB)

Here the second line of each couplet has been indented. Notice how the meaning of each parallels that of the first line of the couplet. A less common form of parallelism used in Hebrew poetry is *antithetical* parallelism, in which the first line makes a statement in a positive way, and the second reinforces it through the negative. An example can be seen in Proverbs 5, as a young man is warned to avoid adulteresses:

> Now, my son, listen to me
>   and do not ignore what I say:
> keep well away from her
>   and do not go near the door of her house;
> (Proverbs 5:7-8, NEB)

There are other forms of parallelism used in Hebrew poetry, but these two examples are enough for now. The point is that the second affirmation in the Lord's prayer is written as a poetic couplet. Jesus prays:

> Thy kingdom come,
>   thy will be done on earth as in heaven.
> (Matthew 6:10, NEB)

In order to fully understand this couplet, we must first look at the words used. The Greek word meaning "kingdom" is *basileia*. The Aramaic word Jesus probably used is *malcootha*. Both words refer to the state of being a king: the dignity, the glory, the power of his reign. Only secondarily do they refer to the territory that he governs. In addition, *malcootha* means "counsel" or "advice." It is derived from the same root as the words meaning "angel" and "counselor". So the image is not of some material "land of God" coming down out of the sky, but rather of the reign or kingship of God becoming real in the hearts and minds of humankind. Now we can see the parallelism of the second line, in which we pray for God's will to be done.

Thy Will be Done

Before we affirm that we want God to rule in our lives, we need to be brutally honest with ourselves. Nothing weakens a prayer life so much as mouthing words that we do not mean.

> Everett had been a Christian for most of his life. He went to church regularly and gave pretty nearly a tithe to its work. He did not drink or smoke, and he loved and spent time with his family. But like many of his Christian friends, he spent a great deal of time fantasizing, daydreaming, and talking about sex. He was never physically unfaithful to his wife, but they both knew that his thoughts as he looked at soft-core pornographic magazines were not what the Lord would want. One evening, Everett and his family went to a concert given by a Christian folksinger. Near the end of the concert, the artist sang a song about the lordship of God in our lives, and how that did not mean that we split our lives

into "His" and "Ours." "God wants all the little kingdoms; He must be Lord *of* all, or He isn't Lord *at* all."

Those words stuck in Everett's mind all the way home and through the next days and weeks. Gradually, as he prayed for God to purify his desires, he was weaned of the addiction to voyeuristic sex. His life became more pure and more whole as he began allowing God's kingdom to come in his own life.

All too often, we say, "Thy will be done," with a sigh of resignation. This is the unregenerate person talking through us. If we carefully read the first chapters of Genesis, we find that the original sin was not eating the fruit, but the human desire to usurp the place of God. It was a statement of "*My* will be done." As we pray, "Thy will be done," we directly repent of that sin in our own lives.

But what of free will? Has God not given us free will for a reason? Free will is a paradox. First, our will both is and isn't free. Many of our desires are rooted not in our own choices but in reaction to our surroundings. Everett would likely have had far less sexual temptation if he had grown up in a time that offered no pornography, or, for that matter, revealing dresses and swimsuits. He would probably have had far more trouble remaining physically faithful to his wife if he had grown up in a family in which extramarital affairs were part of his experience. For this reason, I think that one of the best definitions of free will that I have heard is: "Free will is the ability to focus one's attention." Everett exercised free will, not primarily when he allowed societal pressures to tie his mind up in sexual fantasies, but when he chose to ask God to help him shut out those pressures.

This brings us to the second aspect of the paradox. We often exercise our free will most completely when we voluntarily offer it as a sacrifice to God.

"Have Thine Own Way, Lord" is a hymn that encapsulates much of what inspired Annette's choice to become a missionary to a Third-World nation. When she gave up a secure nursing career at home for the uncertainties of work in a foreign mission field, she felt the sacrifice very keenly. She had lived, worked, and raised her family among those dirt-poor folk for over ten years. But when political unrest forced a long return home, she longed to return to her mission work. She realized that she had a sense of peace and satisfaction about her life, even with all its hardships, that the ease of home could not match. Her choice to let God's will be done in her life turned out not to be a sacrifice at all, in any ultimate sense, but a sensible decision to bow her will freely to God's.

What is God's will for us? Remember that God is Daddy. His will for us is better than whatever we could will for ourselves.

Evan graduated from college with a BS degree and immediately went to work for a large corporation. During his six years with that company, his desire grew to establish his own business. Finally he was able to do so, and for a while he was very happy. But economic conditions declined and Evan, though very honest and creative, was not highly skilled as a business manager. Ultimately the business was forced to close. For about a year, Evan barely made ends meet by doing whatever miscellaneous work he could find. Then one day he heard about an open teaching position. He had never wanted to teach, never even seriously considered teaching, but it would be a steady job. After the first year of teaching had ended, Evan remarked that he had never thought it possible that one could return to work from vacation without a sense of dread and resignation, but that what he felt was enthusiasm. Some ten years later, Evan, still teaching, commented that he still felt the same way. He had come to believe that God wanted him to teach even though Evan himself didn't think he wanted to, and that God used the earlier choices Evan had made to present him with an opportunity to teach at a time when he was likely to accept.

Many times, the desires (whims?) that we array against God's will are not as long-standing as Evan's anti-teaching bias. The importance we attach to our desires of the moment can be downright funny. Like many of us who grew up in the 50's and 60's, I was entranced by cowboy shows on TV. All I wanted for Christmas and birthday presents were toy guns and holsters. I spent many afternoons learning to crack a bullwhip and throw a knife at a target. By the time I was seven, I had discovered that the occupation of old-west United States marshal would not be available to me, so I set my sights on the next-best thing: I decided I would become a modern-day law officer. One day when I was about eleven, I was reflecting on how my preferences had changed from year to year, and I realized with shock that someday I might no longer want to carry a gun and solve crimes and arrest criminals. I could not imagine finding anything that I would enjoy as much as playing marshal. I remember praying earnestly that I might not lose my desire to spend my life in this line of work. Then I discovered the field of electronics. My personal armory in the hall closet was forever abandoned.

Many of our desires are no more appropriate to our real needs than was my desire to become a marshal, and yet we hang onto them with the same laughable tenacity. In my best moments, I recognize that no matter what earthly things or pursuits I may value most highly at a certain time in my life, God may have other plans for me. And those plans will bring me more peace and satisfaction than any plans I could make for myself. In those times, I can sincerely pray, "Thy will be done."

On the other hand, God has given us free will with the expectation that we will use it to make real choices. There are times when we feel no guidance from God about a certain issue.

> Albert was a successful minister of a medium-sized church with a very supportive congregation. He had clearly felt God's leading him to profess faith, and his call to the ministry was also unmistakably clear. Now he had been a minister for about fifteen rewarding years. Then an opportunity came to head an advocacy group for disadvantaged children. He felt very strongly the importance

of the work done by this group, but he also knew the reality of his calling to the parish ministry. Albert and his family prayed constantly for a month, asking for God's guidance in this momentous career choice. But no clear sense of guidance came. Finally Albert was convinced that God's answer was, "You choose. Either path of service is okay with me." He chose the work in child advocacy and his experience since then has proven just as spiritually rewarding as had the pastorate.

Too many times, we think we know what God will answer before we even ask Him. Built into many of us is a silent conviction that if God really had His way with us, we'd all be missionaries to equatorial Africa.

Billy was a young football player with a promising NFL career ahead. But Billy had also been feeling the call of God on his life for some time. During the final minute of the championship game, Billy's team found itself two points behind and on the opponent's thirty-yard line. Knowing that they had slim chance of a touchdown, the coach called for a field-goal kick. Billy was the kicker. As he ran onto the field, feeling the intense pressure, Billy prayed silently to God, "If you'll just let me make this kick so we can win the championship, I'll surrender to You." The kick was good, and Billy soon had the opportunity to follow up on his side of the bargain: he was given a chance to witness to high-school and college athletes about his faith. This opportunity became a regular commitment as Billy worked faithfully in his new mission field. God did not take away his football playing, but instead anointed it with a new meaning and significance.

In fact, Paul speaks clearly about the variety of God's plans for his various persons:

In each of us the Spirit is manifested in one particular way, for some useful purpose. One man through the Spirit, has the gift of wise speech, while another, by the power of the

same Spirit, can put the deepest knowledge into words. Another, by the same Spirit, is granted faith; another, by the one Spirit, gifts of healing, and another miraculous powers; another has the gift of prophecy, and another the ability to distinguish true spirits from false; yet another has the gift of ecstatic utterance of different kinds, and another the ability to interpret it. But all these gifts are the work of one and the same Spirit, distributing them separately to each individual at will.
(1 Corinthians 12:6-11, NEB)

There are equally important but perhaps less "spiritual-sounding" gifts also.

The gifts we possess differ as they are allotted to us by God's grace, and must be exercised accordingly: the gift of inspired utterance, for example, in proportion to a man's faith; or the gift of administration, in administration. A teacher should employ his gift in teaching, and one who has the gift of stirring speech should use it to stir his hearers. If you give to charity, give with all your heart; if you are a leader, exert yourself to lead; if you are helping others in distress, do it cheerfully.
(Romans 12: 6-8, NEB)

Let's look at some real-life examples of "differently gifted" Christians.

Cal served on the staff of a large multifaceted non-profit ministry. Although his degree pointed toward a career as a social worker, most of his work consisted of planning and implementing programs. Cal's co-workers often remarked how smoothly the ministry operated since Cal had come there. On the occasions that Cal was asked to help directly with a client, he felt less fulfilled than when doing his administrative work. Slowly Cal began to realize that his gift of administration should best be used in administration, and that perhaps others were more gifted in social work.

◻ ◻ ◻

Glenice grew up during the Depression, and married Bill shortly after World War II. Bill had a factory job which provided adequately for them and their son, so Glenice stayed home and worked as a mother. She also worked tirelessly in her church. Always a Sunday-School teacher, Glenice was active in the Women's Missionary Union, and there was never a Bible School session at which she was not either a leader or a teacher. After Bill died in the late 1980's, Glenice had sufficient retirement income to live at home and do as she pleased. Instead she chose to teach in her church's child-care center. Through her gift of teaching, she has molded and inspired literally hundreds of young lives.

◻ ◻ ◻

Burton started a textile mill during the 1900's. The mill prospered, and Burton became quite wealthy. Two of his sons continued the business after their father's death; another became a pastor, and the fourth practiced law. All four followed their father's practice of taking seriously their obligation to support the work of their church and denomination. Usually, many more worthy projects asked for their financial support than they could respond to. Yet the brothers regularly met together to plan their contributions as a family. Whenever their church had a major financial need, they could be counted upon to help. The same could be said of the hospitals and colleges supported by their denomination. In the business world, this family was recognized among the leading entrepreneurs of their state, but their Christian calling was lived out through their charity. Not as token givers who seem to feel that they can contribute a little money instead of giving themselves, but as "gifted givers" who also shared their expertise in finance and leadership with their Christian community, this family faithfully exercised their gift.

◻ ◻ ◻

Lana was a journalist. Her popularity as a newspaperwoman, and later as a radio hostess, were due largely to her interest in people and sensitivity to their needs. After retiring, Lana began her own ministry of visiting people in her church, especially those in need, and also sending many little notes and cards through the mail. Although worded as variously as the personalities of their recipients, each card had the same essential message, one that was always deeply appreciated: I love you and appreciate who you are and what you do for your family, the church, the community. Seldom did a week pass without someone stopping Lana on the street or in the church and thanking her, sometimes with tears, for the concern she had so simply expressed. And never did anyone meet Lana without remarking on the joy that shone through her.

◻ ◻ ◻

Melvin had a mechanical bent. Whenever his church needed help with the heating system, or had a plumbing problem, they could count on him to help. He also loved teenagers and worked in the church's youth program and at a nondenominational Christian youth ministry. When he was about thirty, Melvin was elected a deacon. During his first year, he was subjected to a great deal of pressure from the pastor and the chairman of the board of deacons to spend lots of time visiting church members. Each month at their meeting, each deacon was asked to report how many people they had visited during that month. At first Melvin felt a mixture of guilt and anger at this demand. Since he was working both a full-time and a part-time job to support his family and send his wife to college, he was already hard-pressed to give the church the hours for maintenance work and youth ministry. The additional demands of spending his evenings visiting seemed too much. Slowly, Melvin realized that the pastor and the chairman of deacons were suffering from tunnel vision. Both of them were called to the ministry of visiting; neither had gifts in mechanics or youth work. So they understandably but wrongly considered their own strongly felt call to the visiting ministry to be universal. As Melvin came to understand that he was indeed using his own unique gifts for God's work, he also was freed from the guilt of not trying to exercise someone else's gifts also. He began to work through his resentment toward the chairman of deacons, and came to forgive him. Several years later, when the chairman's wife died, Melvin responded by visiting and comforting the lonely old man several times before his passing. Through this whole experience, which spanned many years, Melvin came to appreciate the value and importance of exercising his own gifts, and the error of accepting guilt proffered by others because he was not serving God in some other way.

If we really want to do God's will, we will sincerely seek His guidance. Of course, on most of our decisions, we already know God's will. In many other cases, we can find guidance in the Bible. Doing this requires commitment, however. On some issues, there is a clear commandment: "Thou shalt not kill"; "Thou shalt not commit adultery." But on some questions the Bible does not seem to have clear guidance, and on others, it seems downright contradictory. In these cases, we should begin with a prayer for wisdom.

> If any of you falls short in wisdom, he should ask
> God for it and it will be given him...
> (James 1:5a, NEB)

Wisdom is different from knowledge. Wisdom can be defined as the ability to use knowledge properly. This includes the ability to understand the sense of the Bible on any particular question. That is what we must seek. Too often we "proof-text". We find a certain quotation that we try to apply to many situations. Doing so can be troublesome. First, each Bible passage must be accorded the same courtesy that we would offer any other author's work; it must be considered in context. "A text without a context is a proof-text!" Second, we must take care to find the sense of the entire Bible on the problems that concern us.

> O Babylon, Babylon the destroyer,
>   happy is the man who repays you
>   for all that you did to us!
> Happy is he who shall seize your children
>   and dash them against the rock.
>   (Psalm 137:8-9, NEB)

If we read only these verses, we should conclude that God approves of the most extreme vengeance upon all relatives of our enemies. Jesus provides the corrective for this notion:

> But what I tell you is this: Love your enemies and pray for your persecutors; only so can you be children of your heavenly Father, who makes his sun rise on good and bad alike, and sends the rain on the honest and the dishonest. (Matthew 5:44-45a, NEB)

Getting the sense of the Bible on any question requires a consistent, lifelong study of the Bible. For those who have not spent much time in Bible study, another Christian who is both very honest and a diligent Bible student can be very helpful. This is one important function of a pastor, and one that is underused by many parishioners. But as important as help from other Christians is, it can never replace our personal responsibility to learn as much about God and His ways as we can, and the Bible is the starting point.

Even for long-time Bible students, sometimes there is a problem about which we can't seem to find God's will outlined in the Bible, or about which there seem to be conflicting strands of advice. In these times, prayer for wisdom is essential. Some of us are comfortable finding meaning in our dreams, so we can ask God to send us a dream that shows us His will. Others must have guidance through our rational processes, so we must ask God to help us think and analyze the problem correctly, seeing with His perspective.

> Ariane occasionally seeks guidance by letting the Bible open to whatever page it may happen to, then seeking some

passage that seems to pertain to her current problem. She does this exercise along with prayer for guidance, and only after honestly trying to apply her knowledge of the Bible (gained through many years of patient study) to the issue. She believes that God can control her hands physically in such a way that the Book will open where He wants it to. She can tell of several occasions on which this process has helped her find an answer that proved beneficial, some times when she could find no answer in this way, and no instances of unhelpful advice. I and many other Christians who have talked to Ariane do not find her method helpful at all, but a few do. The important point here is that her approach to "divining" God's will is based upon consistent study of the scripture, prayer, faith, and only then the Bible-opening process. There is no attitude of magic involved, nor is there an attempt to evade spiritual discipline or the responsibility of making the decision.

Once we receive guidance, we may question whether we are really hearing from God, or whether our own imaginations are talking to us. One effective test of guidance is a method that has been called "letting peace be the arbiter." (Colossians 3:15 NEB) Here's what you can do. After seriously seeking guidance from the Bible and through prayer, reduce the problem to a basic one-or-the-other question. Then quiet your mind for a few minutes. Soft instrumental music may help, as may getting away from busy surroundings. While resting in the quiet, propose one of the two answers to the problem. Notice whether you feel an increased or a decreased sense of peace. Try the other solution in the same way. Remember which solution gave you the most peace. Put the problem out of your mind, if possible, for a few hours or overnight. Then enter the silence again and propose the "peaceful" solution again, and then the opposite solution, once again noting which seems to give you more peace. The solution with which you are most nearly at peace is the one most nearly God's will. Like any other human method, this one depends upon our intention to truly seek God's guidance. It will not work if we do not have the dedication to find God's will. It may not produce clear guidance in a choice like Albert's (two equally valid paths of ministry), where God's will is for us to decide on our own. And sometimes we find ourselves so emotionally overwrought that we can not quiet our minds. (In any case, this method takes practice!) But many Christians have found this to be a very helpful method for seeking the will of God.

So as we pray "Thy kingdom come; thy will be done," we affirm that we know God's will is best for our lives, that we desire to know His will for us, and that we intend to act on that will when we understand it. Along with this portion of the Lord's prayer, we may also need to pray for guidance, wisdom, and the strength to do what we know to be right, in the face of habits, fears, or desires to the contrary.

On Earth As In Heaven

The ancients looked at the stars and saw that they moved in inexorable rhythm. Even the planets, which seemed to have meandering paths across the sky (due to their motion being observed from the moving earth, and their proximity to the earth, compared to the stars), nevertheless were predictable in their motions. It was natural for them to assume that the lawful motions of the heavenly bodies stemmed from God's being localized in Heaven. By the dedication of the first temple, Solomon had grown beyond an idea of God that allows Him to be confined to any particular locality:

> But can God indeed dwell on earth? Heaven
> itself, the highest heaven, cannot contain Thee...
> (1 Kings 8:27a, NEB)

Already heaven was becoming a symbol for the Kingdom of God. Where God reigns, all things follow His will. May it be so on earth! Amen!

Give Us This Day Our Daily Bread

What Kind of Bread?

Katherine was overwhelmed. All her life she knew this day would come, and she didn't expect it to be such a big deal. Her father Jerrold had always made it clear that he planned to send her to the finest college available. His emphasis on the importance of education was second only to his love for his family. "Education is food for the mind," he said— a thousand times, Katherine thought. Now here she was, about to embark on the next stage of that lifelong process. Jerrold and Mother Katy had just left (with misty eyes if truth be known), and Katherine had halfway unpacked her belongings when it hit her. Would food be provided for her, or was there to be only the symbolic "food for the mind?"

Do you see how silly this sounds? Preachers and congregations have been choosing sides for almost two thousand years about whether Jesus meant that we should ask God for daily physical food or spiritual food. Those on one side have pointed out that the Lord himself said, "... put away anxious thoughts about food and drink to keep you alive, and clothes to cover your body." (Matthew 6:25a, NEB) And in Matthew 6:32b, Jesus says, "... your heavenly Father knows that you need them all." (NEB) Their opponents responded that Jesus did provide food for the five thousand and the four thousand.

Why must we create an artificial distinction that God does not recognize? The creed of the children of Israel is the Shema, "Hear, O Israel! The LORD is our God, the LORD is One!" (Deuteronomy 6:4, NASB) What is it that He is Lord of? Jesus calls Him Lord of heaven and earth. (Matthew 11:25) Heaven is a symbol for the kingdom of God. Earth is the material world where humans live in flesh bodies. God is Lord of both. We are composite beings: we are spirits, we have souls, and we live in bodies. Our spirits are designed for heaven. Our bodies must live on earth. The spirit gives life to the body. But when the spirit is filled with fear, the body becomes ill. When the body is poisoned with drugs, the spirit is dragged down. Each of us, made in the image of God, is one!

Some of the early Gnostic Christian groups believed that the spirit was incorruptible, and that the body was of no importance. Therefore they taught that nothing that a person did in the flesh mattered, because at death the spirit would return to the heavenly spheres from which it had come. Needless to say, these deluded persons tended to live sordid lives. The larger Christian community soon rejected their ideas. (Before allowing ourselves to be too amazed at this strange belief, we should think for a moment about the number of people we know who are blissfully convinced that they will be rewarded in the afterlife in spite of the dissipation in which they live. In the film *Who Framed Roger Rabbit,* the evil weasel gangsters are killed in the very act of attempting to murder Roger, and their "spirits" are then seen floating heavenward with harps. Light entertainment, yes, but perhaps more true to many people's expectations than we might at first suppose.)

Paul wrote to the Christians at Corinth:

> Surely you know that the unjust will never come into possession of the kingdom of God. Make no mistake: no fornicator or idolater, none who are guilty either of adultery or of homosexual perversion, no thieves or grabbers or drunkards or slanderers or swindlers, will possess the kingdom of God. Such were some of you. But you have been through the purifying waters; you have been dedicated to God and justified through the name of the Lord Jesus and the Spirit of our God.

> "I am free to do anything," you say. Yes, but not everything is for my good. No doubt I am free to do anything, but I for one will not let anything

make free with me. "Food is for the belly and the
belly for food," you say. True; and one day God
will put an end to both. But it is not true that the
body is for lust; it is for the Lord— and the Lord
for the body.
(1 Corinthians 6:9-14, NEB)

We cannot segment our lives into realms of pure spirit and pure
flesh, as though the two were not parts of a whole, any more than we
can pretend that the electrical system of our new car can operate
without the engine keeping the battery charged, or that the engine
can run without the spark plugs and other electrical parts.

Remember to Whom we address our prayers. We are talking to our
Daddy, Who is also El Shaddai! The One who loves us more fully
than we can even love ourselves is also the all-provider! We are to ask
the all-provider for all kinds of food.

Our Work
At the physical level, the prayer for daily bread encompasses many of
the needs we experience in our physical life. Let's look at three
examples.

Adam was an engineer with a successful corporation. He
did his job well and always inspired the younger engineers
by his competence and his positive outlook. In his fifty-
three years, he had held a number of jobs, and his broad
understanding of the engineering field made him a valuable
asset in several local volunteer organizations. He was
looking forward to several more productive years with the
company before retiring to his electronics hobby. Then his
company adopted a new management strategy that required
all plants to compete for highest profit. Because of the
nature of Adam's plant's work, and the segment of the
industry that it served, his plant, along with several others,
was at a disadvantage. When the layoffs came, management
decided to favor the younger employees who had lower
salaries and therefore did not cost as much to retain. Adam
was out of a job.

◻ ◻ ◻

Brandon had felt God calling him to be a pastor, and more specifically, after seminary, he knew he needed to serve as a chaplain in the armed forces. After he had served eight years, his family had developed to the point that he needed a more settled life, so he planned to move into a civilian ministry. He began his work as a counselor for disturbed children. Unfortunately, the instability of funding for organizations that support such positions led to several job changes, and then a position termination. Brandon's problem was not so much the lack of a job as the need for stable work specifically in line with his calling.

◻ ◻ ◻

Sally majored in elementary education, but when she graduated she knew that she really didn't want to teach. In addition, she had a difficult relationship with one of her family members, and the effect of that was to cripple her ability to focus on a career. She was a dedicated Christian who really wanted to help people, but she just didn't know how. Then the traffic accident occurred. With occasional surgery required over a period of several years— including some later surgery to repair the effects of earlier surgery— she really wondered just how she was ever going to be able to prepare for any career, much less find the career that God wanted for her.

Adam, Brandon, and Sally had different concerns, but all of these related to their daily bread. In Genesis, God told a different Adam, "You shall gain your bread by the sweat of your brow until you return to the ground." (Genesis 3:19a, NEB) We have wrongly interpreted this as "the curse of work." In fact, gainful work is a blessing to fallen humanity. How many very rich people do you know of who have no career, yet are happy or productive members of society? How many of these instead wind up in trouble with drugs, alcohol, or shallow, glitzy relationships in a vain attempt to escape an empty life? How well would a child develop if given nothing useful to do, but simply allowed to live in front of TV and video games? Work was divinely ordained, and the loving Daddy who ordained it also wants each of us to find fulfillment in it. The connection of our work with our food is a necessary prod for most of us to attend to our work even when other activities might seem more fun. But this same connection clearly relates all sorts of job concerns to the petition about our daily bread. When we consider the Lord's Prayer as an outline rather than a formula, we find that this section becomes a nest for a great number of our concerns. Adam could pray, "Give us this day our daily bread, and in particular, Lord, help me to find work through which to earn it." Brandon might ask for guidance in finding a specific ministry in which he could earn his daily bread. Sally could ask for resolution of her relationship problems, or at least a level of understanding that would help her move beyond their paralyzing effect. She could also ask for physical healing for her injuries, which were somewhat physically paralyzing, so that she could concentrate on choosing and preparing for the career God had in mind for her.

Our Dependence Upon God

From a broader perspective, the request for daily bread is symbolic of all physical needs. In Matthew 6:25, quoted earlier, Jesus specifically mentions bread and clothing under the same heading. Food, shelter, transportation to and from a place of employment— all these things are appropriate areas of our lives for prayer. The King James translation of Matthew 6:25 says, "Take no thought..." for these things. Christians have sometimes taken this passage to mean that we literally should not think about physical concerns. I once heard a sermon on the radio in which the minister effectively dispelled this notion. He said, " 'Take no thought' doesn't mean 'take no thought'! If you take no thought, you're going to go out and get into your car and drive into a tree. Jesus means, 'Take no *worry* thought'!" The Greek wording is *mē merimnate tē psychē hymōn*, literally, "Do not be anxious for your soul." It does not say, "take no thought." Indeed, we cannot but think about our physical needs; if we entirely gave up thinking about them, we would die, or at least be dependent upon someone to care for us virtually all the time. What we are to do is to remember Who is our source of supply. We are to depend upon God for all these things. One means He uses to meet our needs is our work. But we depend upon Him for the skills with which we work.

Acknowledging our dependence upon God is not easy. On the one hand, we must maintain a high self-esteem and a sense of being in control in order to live a healthy, productive life. On the other hand, considering ourselves to be self-sufficient constitutes pride, to set ourselves in God's place. How do we maintain the balance? Two ideas will help. The first is simply reiterating our dependence upon God as we pray, "Give us this day our daily bread," and mentally reviewing all the provision for which we depend upon Him. It only takes a minute or two for us to be reminded of the givenness of everything. Sometimes we find ourselves resisting the intention to admit this kind of dependence. It is then that we most need the exercise, because at the root of our resistance is, "I can do it all by myself."

The second idea is that while we are not in any sense equal to God, neither are we worms in His sight, as some theologians of the past would have us to believe. He does expect us to work with our hands and minds to make our lives and our world better. He has chosen to enrich His creation with the sons and daughters of humankind, and has given us free will so that we can make creative changes. We can, of course, misuse that free will, but we can also use it properly to make good and constructive changes. The idea of our being co-creators with the One Creator inspires both self-esteem and humility: self-esteem because we are permitted to help shape His creation, and humility because we cannot ever fathom the intricacy of that creation.

Why is it so important that we acknowledge our dependence upon God? Is He so insecure (the Old Testament understanding was that He was jealous) that He needs for us to be very aware of that dependence? How silly! There are very practical reasons why we must acknowledge dependence, the most important being that it is simply true. Jesus promised to send us the Spirit of Truth (John 14:16), and we must therefore embrace truth. Only a very thoroughgoing atheist (if there is any such animal) would believe that he could truthfully claim to live independent of God. Belief in God implies dependence of the entire creation upon Him.

If we depend primarily upon anything or anyone but God, when that thing or person fails us, we will have nothing to fall back upon. The resulting despair is the stuff of which clinical depression and suicides are made. Remembering the story of Brandon, we can see that it would be very easy for him to feel that he was a failure— if he depended primarily upon himself— or that he was forced to work within a hopeless system— if he depended upon those who employ counselors for disturbed children. Happily, though, Brandon "knew in Whom he had believed, and was persuaded that He was able to keep that which he had committed to Him"; his dependence was upon God, and so his disappointing financial circumstances did not cause him to despair.

In fact, Jesus said, "I am that living bread which has come down from heaven; if anyone eats this bread he shall live forever." (John 6:51a, NEB) Shortly after He said this, most of his disciples left Him, because they didn't understand what He was saying. The Twelve didn't understand either, but they depended on Jesus the Man, not on His words, which were often obscure to them. Slowly, they came to realize that bread was a symbol for all that we need— not just all we need physically, but all we need! Jesus, God's representative on earth, represented our total source of supply: spiritual, mental, physical, economic, emotional, and social. In order that we appreciate this fact, God must be very real to us. We cannot *realize* God just by talking about Him, or by studying abstract theology. We begin by thinking about God, but we must immediately progress to experiencing Him by having fellowship with Him through prayer and meditation, talking to Him and praising Him when the many little wondrous things happen in our life, and resting in Him at those times of euphoria and satisfaction. From these times, we draw the strength to depend upon Him when the times seem evil. The realization of God is the basis of faith, "the substance of things hoped for, the evidence of things not seen." (Hebrews 11:1, KJV)

Spiritual Food

Said another way, the realization of God springs from our relationship with God. Relationships must be kept up to date. I have friends with whom I was very close in college, but whom I haven't seen in the last forty-two years. If I were to see these friends again, we would have to spend a good deal of time in relationship-rebuilding before we could approach the old level of intimacy. We cannot realize God if all we have is past experience and future hope; we must experience Him *daily* as present reality. "Behold now is the accepted time; now is the day of salvation." (2 Corinthians 6:2, KJV) This is the spiritual food. This is the Bread of Life.

Often we are told that spiritual food consists of hearing sermons and reading the Bible. I believe that this is only part of the truth. Jesus did not say, "My words are the bread that has come down from heaven," or "People talking about my words are the bread that has come down from heaven." When we take into ourselves (or "eat") the essence of what Jesus was about here on earth, it is spiritual food for us.

Scripture contains two keys to this mystery. The first appears in John chapter 4. One day Jesus and the apostles were hungry, so He sent them ahead to buy bread, while He sat down at Jacob's well outside a Samaritan town called Sychar. A woman of the town came to the well to draw water, and He engaged her in conversation. In order to fully appreciate what happened here, we must first understand that the normal times for drawing water at a public well were early morning and late afternoon, when carrying heavy jars would not be such a hot task. At these times, women would enjoy some social time with each other, which was very important to them. Few of them saw anyone but their children during the day, and they needed the company of other adults.

A woman coming to the well alone at noon would have been one who was a social outcast. As the story progresses, we find out why. The woman had had five husbands, and was living in adultery with yet another man. Clearly she was a woman with a problem! So here is the Jewish rabbi, talking to a despised Samaritan (bad enough), who was a woman (even worse), and of unsavory reputation (worst of all)! Remember that Jesus was fully human; this is what the Incarnation was all about. He was "in all points tempted like as we are." (Hebrews 4:15b, KJV) He had heard from his friends all his life how Samaritans were worthless, how women were only a notch above cattle, and how any self-respecting Jew would certainly avoid talking to women in public, especially women of questionable past. Yet He set all these feelings aside to do God's will. As a result, both the woman and many of her fellow-townspeople were saved. When the disciples returned, they were astounded to find him uninterested in food. Then He told them, "It is meat and drink for me to do the will of him who sent me until I have finished his work." (John 4:34, NEB)

The second key also appears in John, but this time close to the end of Jesus's earthly ministry. During his last recorded prayer with all the apostles before the crucifixion, Jesus asked:

> As thou hast sent me into the world, I have sent them [the apostles] into the world, and for their sake I now consecrate myself, that they too may be consecrated by the truth. But it is not for these alone that I pray, but for those also who through their words put their faith in me; may they all be one: as thou, Father, art in me, and I in thee, so also may they be in us, that the world may believe that thou hast sent me.
> (John 17:19-22, NEB)

Paul said to the Colossians, "The secret is this: Christ in you, the hope of a glory to come." (Colossians 1:27b, NEB) When we eat something, we put it inside us. When Christ really *gets inside* us, we do God's will, and it is meat and drink to us!

Unfortunately, most of us seldom let the Lord get more than a foot in the door, and so we need continual help in taking our spiritual food. Like babies, we cannot seem to eat by ourselves. We are "unskillful in the word of righteousness." (from Hebrews 5:13, KJV) So we need others to help us. These others are the preachers and teachers and writers, both writers of the Bible and writers of present-day books and articles. Even the fellowship of other "ordinary"

Christians helps to strengthen us and give us the will to eat at God's table.

If we are to pray for God's help concerning our physical food, we are certainly to pray concerning our spiritual food also. The experience of two young Christians will serve as examples.

> Jeanne graduated from college with a degree in elementary education. Her first job was in a small southern town not unlike the one in which she had grown up. Immediately upon moving into an apartment, Jeanne began to look for a church. She had grown up in a very conservative country church, and had been very comfortable in it. But during her years in college, she began to sense a need for answers to some questions to which her church training gave her no clue. She was very active in her denomination's college-student organization, and she especially enjoyed the retreats on which she could discuss her questions and interpretations of the Bible in the light of her own growing understanding and that of her fellow students. The college chaplain always guided the discussions, but he also was open to new insights. On the other hand, Jeanne had known students who claimed to be Christian, but whose life-style gave no evidence of it. These folk considered themselves to be free-minded and modern, but to Jeanne, they were simply self-deluded. Now Jeanne wanted to find a church in which the elements of peer discussion and openness among the church leaders were prominent, but also one in which the true essence of the Christian faith was preserved.

口 口 口

> Shawn grew up in a very formal church, and in his mind, the church was not about any particular set of teachings so much as it was a place of comforting rituals. He had gone to a denominational college, and none of his experiences there had made much change in his ideas of what a church should be. After graduation, Shawn drifted away from church,

attending only when he went home to visit his family. When his girlfriend of many years suddenly dropped him, he found himself without a sense of direction. His performance at work suffered. One of his friends noticed it and invited Shawn to his church. It was his first experience in a charismatic church, and the openness and warmth of the people attracted him, as did the spontaneity of the worship. For the first time in his life, Shawn felt that he really was worshipping, rather than just engaging in dry rituals. But seeing his friend and others begin "speaking in tongues" frightened Shawn. He knew that here was something different and powerful, but he was not sure if it was good for him.

Both Jeanne and Shawn faced real problems related to their spiritual food. Church provides a support structure for Christians, and equally important, it opens opportunities to serve. Along with books and teaching CD's and other guides, church also can provide stimulating spiritual teaching to more fully engage our mental faculties in our spiritual growth. Church helps keep us centered, and should help us avoid being drawn away from God by earthly concerns. Fellow-Christians in church can help us through the dry seasons in our lives when we seem to have trouble meeting with God. But as each of us is an individual, so each has individual needs to be met by a church family. Finding a church that meets our needs and provides us with opportunities for service is extremely important. Therefore, we, along with Jeanne and Shawn, are to pray about our choice of churches and church activities, which help us to take our spiritual food, as we ask for our daily bread.

And Forgive Us our Offenses, as We Forgive Our Offenders

The Greek word *kai*, translated *and*, really is a part of this line of the Lord's Prayer. Therefore this petition is the second half of a sentence, and admittedly we do some violence to the continuity of the prayer by treating it separately. However, the emphasis has shifted from that in the first part of Jesus's sentence, so I have chosen to examine the two parts individually. In doing so, though, we must always remember that Jesus expressed a clear link between our forgiving others and our receiving our daily bread! Certainly we must not jump to a Deuteronomic theology that says everyone who obeys the Law will be financially well-off, while all who disobey will be poor. The connection is with our spiritual daily bread. Unforgiveness on our part blocks our relationship with God. How can a mean and unforgiving creature commune with a loving and forgiving Creator? In forgiving, we do not change God's mind about us; we change ourselves so that we can truly call God Daddy, and relate to Him as such.

Offenses

About half of the readers of this book would be glad to see the word *debts* in the title of this chapter, and the other half will wonder why *trespasses* or *sins* was not used. The Greek word is *opheilemata*, which literally means debts or obligations. Only in this passage do the translators of the New Testament seem to use this word as a synonym for "sin". When we do wrong, or fail to do right, we establish a need for repayment. Often that need is addressed toward a human brother or sister. Clearly if I steal from you, I owe you your goods in return. According to the Law, I also owe you punitive damages (see Exodus 22:1, Leviticus 6:4-5, and Numbers 5:7). In fact, when King David was faced with a hypothetical theft of a lamb from a poor man, he judged that the lamb should be repaid fourfold (2 Samuel 12:6). As part of his repentance, Zaccheus offered to repay anyone he cheated fourfold (Luke 19:8). If we genuinely repent of the sin of theft, or any other sin that can humanly be repaid, we will make restitution. It is less clear how we can repay other sin-debts, such as murder, slander (bearing false witness), and adultery. When the Holy Spirit convicts us of sins like these, we still feel a sense of indebtedness, but a great part of the damning ability of these sins is our inability to undo what we have done— to make restitution for these debts.

Jesus said, "Anything you did [or did not do] for one of my brothers here, however humble, you did [or did not do] for me." (Matthew 25:40b [and 45], NEB) So when we sin against a fellow human, we also sin against our Lord.

There are other sins that are specifically against God, not humans. The first two commandments are:

> Thou shalt not have other gods, besides me.
> Thou shalt not make to thee an image of any
> form, that is in the heavens above, or that is in
> the earth beneath, or that is in the waters beneath
> the earth: thou shalt not bow thyself down to
> them, nor be led to serve them.
> (Exodus 20 :3-5a, Rhm)

These two commandments are essentially the same. They are about idolatry. Clearly this sin is a great offense against God, for it is the only one that merited two separate commandments. Idolatry was one of the chronic sins of the Hebrews throughout the time of the Old Testament. It was always a case of, "But Daddy, everybody else is doing it!" The warning against intermarrying with non-Hebrews was given primarily to avoid what happened even to the "wise" Solomon:

> King Solomon was a lover of women, and
> besides Pharoah's daughter he married many
> foreign women, Moabite, Ammonite, Edomite,
> Sidonian, and Hittite, from the nations with

> whom the LORD had forbidden the Israelites to
> intermarry, "because," he said, "they will entice
> you to serve their gods". But Solomon was
> devoted to them and loved them dearly. He had
> seven hundred wives, who were princesses, and
> three hundred concubines, and they turned his
> heart from the truth. When he grew old, his
> wives turned his heart to follow other gods, and
> he did not remain wholly loyal to the LORD his
> God as his father David had been.
> (1 Kings 11:1-4, NEB)

The result was that the kingdom was divided. Solomon was not the
first son of Israel to commit idolatry, and he was certainly not the
last. It was not until the bitter medicine of the Babylonian exile had
been administered that the overt sin of idol-worship was finally
purged from the nation.

Why does idolatry concern God so much? Surely He can understand
that humans have limited knowledge and that we make mistakes.
After all, how can He really need our worship? First of all, remember
that we are talking about our Daddy, and it hurts Him to be
abandoned. How would your earthly father have felt if you had
"adopted" some other man as your father, or even as a co-father?
Second, God knows that we become like that which we worship. If
we worship Molech, who was believed to be a god who ate children,
then we sacrifice our children to Molech, so that our crops will
provide food for us. Thus, in a very real sense, we also eat our
children. If we worship Baal, who was a fertility god, we patronize
temple prostitutes as an act of worship. The effect of this practice
upon family life and public morality, not to mention public health,
was tragic. If we worship Yahweh, we become more loving. Now
which form of worship would you want for your children?

Books have been written on the subject of modern idolatry. Some of
us are so devoted to our jobs that we sacrifice our children on the
altar of success. Some of us are so devoted to sex that we worship at
the idol of our local theater (or even at our TV in our own living
room. The nations surrounding the Hebrews had "house gods" in

their homes too!) Many of us are so devoted to sports that we sacrifice most of our family life in honor of our god.

> Ned had a very real revelation of his personal idolatry. Although he considered himself a good Christian husband and father, he had a roving eye. When he walked around town, or when he watched a play or a movie or a TV show, he was always alert to the bodies of women. In his mind, he undressed a dozen women every day. He never acted upon his fantasies, but the lust was a major part of his life. One night, Ned had a dream in which he was looking at a particularly voluptuous nude woman. As he did so, he heard himself saying over and over, "Oh, my god, oh, my god!" When he awakened the next morning, he realized that the real God had used this dream to call him back from idolatry. The change did not come suddenly, but gradually Ned was able to refocus his thoughts and place God back in the center of his life. At their foundation, all sins against God are sins of idolatry, in that they represent our placing someone or something other than God in the most prominent position in our lives.

Now we can see that sin is more serious than just a debt that we can repay. Sin is more than a "trespass," which just means that I have walked on your land. It is an offense against our fellow-human, and it is also an offense against our loving Daddy. But He loves us so much that He forgives our offenses.

The Greek *aphiēmi* means "forgive," "release," or "untie". When God forgives us, He releases us from the trap of our sins. How are they a trap? Well, aside from the habit-forming nature of many sins, there is a more insidious entrapment: guilt. When we sin, we know it, and we feel guilty. The intensity of the guilt depends upon a great many things, but there is always guilt. Often, it seems down deep inside that we *should* feel guilty, as a way of making up for sinning. Subconsciously we feel that we absolve ourselves of guilt if we feel bad enough about our sin. This feeling is a lie of Satan. All that guilt accomplishes is to make us feel separated from God. When we feel separated from God, we are at best uncomfortable asking forgiveness. This leads to unrepentance, which adds to our feeling of unworthiness. The emotional strain weakens our judgment and our resistance to temptation. Then we sin some more. More guilt, etc.

Being Forgiven

God has chosen to break this downward spiral by freely forgiving us, untying, loosening, and releasing us from the net of sin. Somehow we Christians have gotten the idea that God is so pure that He can't behold sin, and therefore, He has this record book in which He keeps a list of all our sins. Then when we feel good and sorry for our sins, He tears out the page and we begin anew. This is wrong in several ways. First, God is so pure that only He *can* behold sin and not fall to temptation. He (in Jesus) "was in all points tempted like as we are, yet without sin." (Hebrews 4:15, KJV) He is so pure that He (in Jesus) became sin for us, "that in him we might be made one with the goodness of God Himself." (Hebrews 5:21b, NEB) Second, God doesn't need to keep a record of our sins, as though anything we could do would ever repay them. Something God has done long ago has already taken care of our sins. Third, feeling good and sorry is not a part of the deal. Jesus tells of only two preconditions for forgiveness: that we repent and that we forgive others.

Repentance has nothing to do with feeling sorry or tearing out your hair or ripping your clothes or wearing sackcloth and ashes. To repent (Greek *metamelomai*) is to turn around and go the other way. When we decide to leave sin behind, we are repenting. At that point, we should be feeling intense joy, because we know we have been forgiven, and we know we are doing God's will. "Sorry" has no part in the matter. Repentance is necessary, though, because God honors our free will and won't release us from sin that we insist upon holding onto.

Forgiving Others

"... As we forgive our offenders." Ah, there's the rub! Jesus leaves no doubt that forgiveness is required of us. His words in the Lord's Prayer alone are enough. But there is more.

> You have learned that our forefathers were told,
> "Do not commit murder; anyone who commits

> murder must be brought to judgment." But what
> I tell you is this: Anyone who nurses anger
> against his brother must be brought to judgment.
> (Matthew 4:21-22a, NEB)

Nursing anger is the opposite of forgiving; it is a blatant refusal to release the brother from blame for the real or perceived sin.

> For if you forgive others the wrongs they have
> done, your heavenly Father will also forgive you;
> but if you do not forgive others, then the wrongs
> you have done will not be forgiven by your
> Father.
> (Matthew 6:14-15, NEB)

The preceding passage appears in Matthew immediately after the Lord's Prayer, almost as a commentary.

> The kingdom of Heaven, therefore, should be
> thought of in this way: There was once a king
> who decided to settle accounts with the men
> who served him. At the outset there appeared
> before him a man whose debt ran into millions.
> Since he had no means of paying, his master
> ordered him to be sold to meet the debt, with his
> wife, his children, and everything he had. The
> man fell prostrate at his master's feet. "Be patient
> with me," he said, "and I will pay in full"; and the
> master was so moved with pity that he let the
> man go and remitted the debt. But no sooner had
> the man gone out than he met a fellow-servant
> who owed him a few pounds; and catching hold
> of him he gripped him by the throat and said,
> "Pay me what you owe." The man fell at his
> fellow-servant's feet, and begged him, "Be
> patient with me, and I will pay you"; but he
> refused, and had him jailed until he should meet
> the debt. The other servants were deeply
> distressed when they saw what had happened,

and they went to their master and told him the whole story. He accordingly sent for the man. "You scoundrel!" he said to him; "I remitted the whole of your debt when you appealed to me; were you not bound to show your fellow-servant the same pity as I showed you?" And he was so angry that he condemned the man to torture until he should pay the debt in full. And that is how my heavenly Father will deal with you, unless you each forgive your brother from your hearts.
(Matthew 18:23-35, NEB)

Jesus used strong words to evoke responses from His listeners. We have a problem with the idea of a loving God condemning us to torture. But let's look carefully at this idea. One way of teaching children is through natural and logical consequences. A child will never learn if we always make all his choices for him. There are times when we must say, "Go ahead, then; you'll see for yourself why I said not to touch the hot stove!" The child's free will has been exercised by him and honored by us, and the lesson that we tried so hard to teach verbally has been learned quickly and effectively through pain. We cannot be said to have caused the child's pain. Indeed, in more serious matters we will intervene to prevent the pain from being too serious for the child. But sometimes, experience is not only the best, but the only teacher a child will listen to. We are much the same. God honors our free will so much that He allows our refusal to forgive to produce a state of mind in us that blocks our relationship with Him. Living outside of relationship with God is torture; not, of course, the sort the Inquisitors used, but a longer-lasting, draining kind of torture. God, too, feels this torture when His children fall out of relationship with Him. But He will not override our free will. Therefore, when we choose actions whose natural and logical consequences bring torture upon us, He must allow it.

Not only does our being forgiven depend upon our forgiving, but all other aspects of our relationship with God depend upon it also. Kenneth Copeland tells of a time when he was in a spiritual desert. He had trouble receiving guidance from God, and when he prayed, it seemed as though he was talking to the ceiling. He took time aside one day to pray specifically about this problem. That night, he had a dream in which he saw a large pipeline extending from heaven to a point just above his head. He could see that huge amounts of water were flowing into the pipeline, but only a tiny trickle emerged at the bottom. In the dream, he asked what was blocking the pipeline, and he heard one word: "unforgiveness". The next morning, he was working with the dream, and he asked God to reveal the areas in which he was failing to forgive. Suddenly images began coming to his mind: there was the cafeteria server who had put gravy on his mashed potatoes when he had just asked her not to; there was the person who had cut him off in traffic. He got the picture. Often it is not the large things that cause trouble, but the many small slights and injuries that we never remember to forgive.

What makes our forgiving so important to God? We are all God's family. In an earthly family, any good father or mother will be hurt when the children do not get along. Most often when this happens, the trouble stems from something so petty that it does not matter. Petty, that is, seen from the parent's point of view. But from each child's point of view, at least at the time, the matter is of great importance. Therefore setting aside self enough to forgive is difficult for the child. But as long as this does not occur, the family relationship is crippled. Even those not involved in the dispute have to tread carefully when they relate to the disputants. Only forgiveness will make the family relationship whole again.

There's more. Let's say that Johnny took Janet's stuffed bear. Human justice would say that Johnny is in the wrong and should suffer for his misdeed, while Janet has been wronged and should be consoled. However, as long as Janet does not forgive Johnny, her anger remains a festering wound within her. She who will not forgive suffers equally with the offender. By her unforgiveness, she has locked herself in the same jail with him. An old Welsh proverb says that it takes two to make a prisoner: the jailed and the jailer. Neither can escape if the prisoner is to remain imprisoned. If Janet forgives Johnny— whether he repents or not— then she can walk away from the jail and be free. Her forgiveness may prompt Johnny to repentance. But even if it does not, that is now his problem, not hers. She has done her part in restoring the family relationships to wholeness.

Sin cripples relationships. When we have sinned, we must turn around— repent— in order to restore the relationship. When others sin against us, we must forgive them, else our very unforgiveness is sin. Why must we forgive even when our offender does not repent, yet it seems that God only forgives us when we repent?

Perhaps it would be more accurate to say that we cannot receive the benefit of God's forgiveness unless we repent. As long as we do not acknowledge a wrong that we have done, we cannot acknowledge any need of forgiveness for it, and therefore we cannot acknowledge the forgiveness itself. In fact, nowhere in the Bible is repentance given as a precondition for God's action in forgiving us. But without repentance, the forgiveness will have no reality for us, so from our point of view, we may as well not be forgiven. And if we do not turn away from our sins, we go on sinning. So repentance is necessary for our spiritual growth and attunement with God, even though we may be forgiven without it. So there really is no paradox. Even if our brother sins against us on seventy times seven occasions (see Matthew 18:22), we are to forgive him. Clearly this habitual sinning does not include repentance. And if we commit seventy times seven sins against God, He forgives us. But if Johnny keeps on taking Janet's bear, even if she is able to always forgive him, he still has a canker in his heart toward her because of his guilt, until he repents and stops sinning against her. Janet's forgiveness frees her, but only Johnny's repentance frees him!

> Mabel's mother was a social worker. Her job kept her away from the house most days and many evenings. When the housework began to pile up, she took the only way out that she had energy to take: she told Mabel and her older brother Hank to clean up. The three younger children were almost never asked to help, not out of a lack of fairness, but simply because enforcing the request and providing the necessary guidance and follow-up with the younger children would have taken more energy than Mabel's mother had. So Mabel grew up with a fermenting anger toward her mother

because it seemed that she always had to work, while the younger kids took it easy. After Mabel moved away from home, she became a Christian, and she saw the need to forgive her mother. But try as she might, she could not seem to succeed. In fact, the more she tried to forgive, the more it seemed that the old anger surged up.

Have you ever had an experience like Mabel's? Why must it be so hard to forgive? In fact, it is not. But there are common misunderstandings that short-circuit our efforts to forgive. The first is a misunderstanding of what forgiving, and indeed loving, are all about. Let's look at love first, for the ability to forgive flows from the ability to love. There are several Greek words for love. The one that Jesus used when He commanded that we love one another is the same one that Paul defined in 1 Corinthians 13: *agape.* Listen to his explanation:

> Love is patient; love is kind and envies no one.
> Love is never boastful, nor conceited, nor rude;
> never selfish, not quick to take offense. Love
> keeps no score of wrongs; does not gloat over
> other men's sins, but delights in the truth. There
> is nothing love cannot face; there is no limit to its
> faith, its hope, and its endurance.
> (1 Corinthians 13:4-7, NEB)

Notice that nowhere are warm, fuzzy feelings mentioned, nor blistering passion, nor any of the other emotions that we commonly associate with the word *love.* In fact, emotion has little to do with this kind of love. The King James Version of the Bible used the word *charity,* or selfless giving, instead of *love,* to translate *agape.* This kind of love is characterized by an impersonal desire for the best possible things to happen to other persons. We can hold, and act upon, this desire, even when we do not like the other person. In fact, nowhere are we given the command to like anyone. But we are to love everyone. Certainly it is easier to love someone whom we like. But the love comes first.

Try this exercise sometime. Select someone whom you particularly dislike. This should be a person who is a part of your everyday life, not a public character whom you know only through others' descriptions. We will call him Percival. Each day or night as you pray, offer specific prayers for Percival. Start with a very general prayer, such as, "God, Percival is your child even as I am; please enable him to experience only those things that are for his ultimate good and keep evil from his door." As you do this, you will no doubt find more specific objects for your prayers for Percival: his health, his job, his family life. After about six months, compare your feelings toward Percival. I think you will find that you are beginning to like him, or that at least your dislike for him has moderated. Of course you may still disapprove of many things about Percival, but by exercising love toward him, you will be drawn to appreciate him as a person. Use this exercise carefully, or you may wind up with Percival as a treasured friend!

Did you notice that according to Paul, "Love keeps no score of wrongs"? Love is forgiving. Therefore the technique of forgiving is much like the technique for *agape* loving. What is required first is the will to forgive. We can never develop this will by remembering the wrong. But neither can we forget just by choosing to do so.

Like many spiritual disciplines, choosing to forgive first occurs at the mental level. The trick is to make it real at the emotional level also. This can be accomplished if we use the principle of replacement. We replace the thoughts of having been wronged with thoughts of how much God has forgiven us. Then we can remember that the person who has offended us (Percival again?) is also a child of God. Even when we feel most uncharitable toward this person, we can still admit this truth. At this point, we simply say (either mentally or aloud), "I freely choose to forgive Percival for whatever wrong he has committed toward me." The sin does not even need to be named; in fact, it may be better not to name it, since we are busy replacing it in our consciousness. Then we briefly pray for God's blessing on Percival and turn our mind to other things. It is most important at this point to move the mental focus to something else. From time to time, thoughts of anger and/or resentment may creep up on us, and we find ourselves slipping back into unforgiveness. At these times, just offer another prayer of blessing for Percival and focus once again on something else of importance to you. Soon these thoughts will come less frequently, and then, not at all. One day, some event may bring the wrong to mind and we will be amazed at the absence of bitterness, for the forgiveness is complete.

There are several pitfalls to be avoided. The first was already mentioned: we must not allow ourselves to concentrate on the wrong. Use the principle of replacement to cast it from your mind. The second is to avoid the temptation to despair when the feeling of anger resurfaces. This does not mean we have failed to forgive; it simply means that our emotions have not yet gotten the message. Likewise, we do not need to repeat the act of forgiveness. To do this is tacitly to tell our own subconscious that it "didn't take" the first time, which of course implies that it may not take the second time either. We cannot reprogram our subconscious to dissociate angry feelings from the memory of the event as long as we show no confidence in our own ability to forgive and love Percival. Finally, when the feeling of release from our chain of unforgiveness comes, we must avoid the temptation of probing back to remember just how the anger and bitterness felt! It is a sad fact that negative emotions have a hook that makes them difficult for us to release. This is true of anger, grief, melancholy, depression, and many other feelings that we seldom admit to liking. Therefore, when we try to release any of these feelings, we need to be vigilant against abetting their return by mentally reviewing the events that triggered them.

Periodically, each of us needs to examine our relationships and see if there is anyone against whom we are carrying a grudge, anyone whom we have not forgiven. Praying for God to bring any unforgiveness to our attention is quite in order. As soon as we find that we are holding on to some cherished slight, we must immediately begin the process of forgiveness. The cost of failing to do so is far too great.

Forgiving Ourselves

Jesus said, "Judge not, that ye be not judged; for with what judgment ye judge shall ye be judged." (Matthew 7:1, Rhm) We usually apply His commandment to questions of our judgment of others, and rightly so. But, many modern translations to the contrary, the Greek does not include any specific mention of "others". It is also true that we are not to judge ourselves. Paul said, "I do not even pass judgment on myself .... My Judge is the Lord." (1 Corinthians 4:3, NEB) When God has forgiven us, we are forgiven. To continue to feel guilt is to judge ourselves, and to reject His forgiveness. It may even feel very holy to say, "Oh, I am not worth forgiving. Maybe I haven't really repented. Maybe I've committed the unforgivable sin," etc. In fact, these thoughts are very self-centered, faithless, and dangerous. They are self-centered and faithless because they give more credence to how we feel than to God's Word. Jesus said, "... if you forgive others the wrongs they have done, your heavenly Father will also forgive you" (Matthew 6:14, NEB). How we feel has nothing to do with the matter. These thoughts are dangerous because they block our communion with God. Receiving forgiveness, or forgiving ourselves, is a crucial part of the process about which Jesus told us to pray.

Many Christians through the ages have wondered just what the "unforgivable sin" is, and have feared that they may have committed it. The Scripture passage that prompts most of the questions is Mark 3:29 (and its parallel in Luke 12:10): "I tell you this: no sin, no slander, is beyond forgiveness for men; but whoever slanders the Holy Spirit can never be forgiven; he is guilty of eternal sin." (NEB) The context of this passage is that Jesus was casting out evil spirits and healing people, and the doctors of the law said that He was possessed by Beelzebub. The next verse is, "He said this because they had declared that he was possessed by an unclean spirit." (Mark 3:30, NEB) So Jesus's statement was a specific response to those who had seen the clear work of the Spirit and had declared it to be of the devil. If we reject the work of the Holy Spirit, then that Spirit can have no part in our lives, because God will not override our free will. C. S. Lewis pointed out that one of the works of the Holy Spirit is to convict us of our sins, so that we may repent. (See John 16:8-11) If we deny the Spirit that work in our lives, then we do not repent, and therefore cannot receive forgiveness. This argument is strengthened by Jesus's statement in Luke 12:10a: "Anyone who speaks a word against the Son of Man will receive forgiveness... " (NEB). The limitation of unforgiveness to one person of the Trinity leads us to the conclusion that it is in fact the function of that person in our salvation that cannot be denied without rescinding the salvation. In the very act of praying Jesus's prayer to a loving Daddy, we affirm the power and goodness of God, and, by implication, of the Holy Spirit, who "through our inarticulate groans... is pleading for us, and God who searches our inmost being knows what the Spirit means, because He pleads for God's people in God's own way" (Romans 8:26b-27, NEB).

And Lead Us to Avoid Temptation; Save Us from the Evil

Whoa, here! That's not what the Lord's Prayer says, at least, none of the versions that I have ever heard!

Just what do the familiar versions say?

> Lead us not into temptation, but deliver us from evil. (Matthew 6:13, KJV)

But James, the younger half-brother of our Lord, says:

> No one under trial or temptation should say, "I am being tempted by God"; for God is untouched by evil, and does not himself tempt anyone. Temptation arises when a man is enticed and lured away by his own lust; then lust conceives, and gives birth to sin; and sin full-grown breeds death.
> (James 1:13-15, NEB)

Even if we did not have this clear word from Scripture, we would have great difficulty understanding how a loving Daddy could tempt us to do evil, or why He must be requested not to lead us into temptation.

The problem this time does not lie in any obscurity in the translation from Greek to English, but rather in finding a way to phrase the idea in English. Let us consider alternative English wordings. If we say, "Lead us not into temptation," we imply that God might otherwise lead us into temptation. If we say "Lead us from temptation", we imply that temptation is already there, like a sand-trap on some cosmic golf course, and we are asking God to help us avoid it. But James says otherwise: temptation does not arise until we are enticed and lured by our own lust. If we say, "Do not let us enter into temptation" we are asking that God actively prevent us from doing something which we may choose to do, and God does not override our free will.

What we have here is a concept that is very easy to understand, but quite difficult to put into words. So Jesus stated it in a poetic couplet, and the second line of the couplet clarifies the first. "But deliver us from the evil." Certainly evil is all around us, and it is from this evil— from its attacks on us, and from our participation in its work— that we want to be delivered. This is a prayer of protection. We recognize our dependence upon God even to the extent that we must be helped to choose what we really want! Paul puts it this way:

> I do not even acknowledge my own actions as mine, for what I do is not what I want to do, but what I detest. But if what I do is against my will, it means that I agree with the law and hold it to be admirable. But as things are, it is no longer I who perform the action, but sin that lodges in me. For I know that nothing good lodges in me— in my unspiritual nature, I mean— for though the will to do good is there, the deed is not... .

> I discover this principle, then: that when I want to do the right, only the wrong is within my reach... .

> Miserable creature that I am, who is there to rescue me from this body doomed to death? God alone, through Jesus Christ our Lord! Thanks be to God!
> (Romans 7:15-18, 21, 24b-25a, NEB)

When we surrender our will to God for our overall life's direction, we allow Him to work within us to help us to avoid being enticed and lured by our lusts. Whether we translate the Greek *ponērou* as "evil," "the evil," or "the evil one," the sense is the same. Evil is real. Our danger of falling into evil is real. We are not perfect; in fact, as Paul says, our remaining unspiritual nature contains nothing good. We need help. Jesus says we should ask God for that help, since He alone can give it.

Socrates said that a good person cannot be harmed by an evil person. Was he right? On the surface, most of us would be tempted to point to Socrates' own untimely end as a counter-example of this statement. But the old philosopher himself would say that his death was not a triumph of evil over good, because his essence was not the physical body, which was all that they could kill. (In fact, I think he would argue that he gave his life; it was not taken from him. See Plato's account of Socrates' last discourses.)

But Socrates was arguing from the Greek point of view, which separates the spirit from the body. This is not the Christian understanding. Just as we know God as Father, Son, and Holy Spirit, we know ourselves as spirit, soul, and body. Both our understanding of God and our understanding of ourselves is trinitarian. This does not necessarily imply that the physical body is a permanent part of our being; in fact, Paul discusses the interplay of body and spirit in the afterlife at some length in 1 Corinthians 15. But we Christians will not claim that an injury to the body is unimportant. At the least physical injuries— and for that matter, injuries to, or loss of, our property— are inconvenient. Is it true then that we need protection not only from the temptation to do evil, but also from evil attacks on ourselves, our families, and our possessions?

Some Christians claim that anything that happens to us is according to the will of God. They believe that if God is all-powerful, then nothing can happen without its being His will. Following this thinking to its logical conclusion must either make God the author of evil, or else must claim that evil is illusory: it is just part of a larger good that we cannot comprehend. In order to avoid this conclusion, some theologians have come up with the idea of God's *permissive* will. Evil things happen because God permits them, even though they are not His best will for us. These ideas are based on an Old-Testament (i.e., incomplete) understanding of God. To have all power does not imply the necessity of using all power. The ancient Hebrews failed to notice this fact, and built much of their theology around a fallacy. So they wrote sentences like, "The spirit of the LORD had forsaken Saul, and at times an evil spirit from the LORD would seize him suddenly." (1 Samuel 16:14, NEB) They thought that if God exercised all power, and an evil spirit came upon Saul, then it must be from God. But James said, "God is untouched by evil." (from James 1:13, NEB) There is no call to try to reconcile these two sayings from Scripture. The entire Bible is a record of God's progressive self-revelation to mankind, and that process had not progressed as far when 2 Samuel was written as it had by the time James wrote. God created humanity for a purpose that is not specifically stated in the Bible, but reading between the lines, we come to think that it was for companionship. God does not need robots or stuffed animals or dolls. Therefore, He gave His people free will, and in doing so, God deliberately limited His own power. Our free will is so very real that we can even will to be eternally separated from our Creator, and He will honor that will. It is so very real that we can choose to harm other people, and He will honor that will. The fall of humanity, and the subsequent falls of each member of mankind, result from abuse of this free will. The Bible makes it very clear that there are other orders of created beings besides humans. Apparently at least some of them have abused their free will also, because Peter warns us that, "Your enemy the devil, like a roaring lion, prowls around looking for someone to devour." (1 Peter 5:8, NEB) God's creation is working toward a culmination in which we will all exercise our free will to be one with Him, as Jesus prayed in the last part of John 17. (This is not the place to debate just who is included in the "we" who will be one with God, which is ultimately God's business and not ours anyway, for who are we to judge another's servant? [*cf* Romans 14:4]) Therefore, evil is real, not illusory, and we can harm one another, though not in an eternal sense. Are we then defenseless against beings seen and unseen who would do evil to us? Certainly not! Our defense is in God.

Now at this point you may be feeling the gentle lull of your Sunday-School hat sliding down comfortably onto your head, surrounding your brain with fog. Stop it! Many, if not most of us who have been Christian for some time have learned a very insidious way of ignoring the truth of God when it does not echo the ideas of the *Zeitgeist*. At any place and time in human history, there are certain attitudes that are held by most people, and which are so much a part of society that they are not noticed. Plato clearly saw this phenomenon, and he described it in his famous story about the cave.

> There was a group of people who spent their lives sitting in a cave, facing the back wall. Each day, they saw shadows of people passing outside the cave, but since they could not see the people, their entire reality was made up of shadows. One day, several of the group were allowed to turn around and see the real world. When they came back to describe their experiences to their friends, they were rejected as insane, since their enlightened experience was contrary to the shadowland that their compatriots had known.

Each community of humans has its own shadowland, and the lore of that land forms the background beliefs against which their experiences are measured. German philosophers have called these beliefs the *Zeitgeist*, or the spirit of the age. As Christians, we have glimpsed the world outside the cave. Much of that world is discussed in the Bible. But we shy away from really believing parts of the Bible that are not confirmed by the *Zeitgeist*, lest we be condemned as insane, or as religious fanatics, or perhaps even because we are not willing to take the leap of faith that says, "I will believe what Scripture says to me, even if I stand alone in that belief." Of course we will not stand alone, and the witness of others on the same quest in fact helps us to understand what Scripture does say. Yet this is a frightening stance, because it demands severe honesty with ourselves and extreme dedication to the spiritual life. So we put on our Sunday-school hats and say of Scripture, "Well, that's all very well, but it won't work in the real world." Or we say, "Yes, but church is church and business is business"; or, "Things were different in Bible times"; or, "So much of that is symbolic or deals with old superstitions, and we know better today." We have many ways of ignoring God's word without admitting to ourselves that we are doing so. Thus we stay "respectable".

It is not very respectable today to believe in spiritual adversaries, but Paul said:

> Our fight is not against human foes, but against cosmic powers, against the authorities and

> potentates of this dark world, against the
> superhuman forces of evil in the heavens.
> (Ephesians 6:12, NEB)

He was not speaking figuratively. He was saying to the Christians at Ephesus, "It is not the Romans who are bent on persecuting you, but spiritual forces of evil who merely use the Romans as tools."

We are not to consider any human as our enemy. Other people may act as enemies, but we are to love them. They may try to do evil to us, but we are to forgive them and pray for them. And we are to pray for God to deliver us and separate us and set us free from the evil.

At the same time, we are to stay out of evil's way. Jesus said, "Look, I send you out as sheep among wolves; be wary as serpents, innocent as doves." (Matthew 10:16, NEB) Serpents do not sneak out of their holes and lie in wait to attack people. They try mightily to stay out of harm's way. Only when cornered will they attack. Jesus didn't say that we should attack like serpents, but that we steer clear of evil. We can do this at the physical level. Nowhere does the Bible mention avoiding drug abuse, but certainly if we abuse drugs, we place ourselves directly in harm's way. The law of cause and effect is one of the tools that God uses to help us learn, and if we set the cause of drug abuse in motion, we will experience the effect of physical, mental, and emotional degradation. If we set the cause of sexual license in motion, we will experience the effect of relational and emotional and perhaps physical degradation. If we set the cause of gluttony in motion, we will experience the effect of physical and perhaps emotional and even financial degradation.

We can also steer clear of evil at the spiritual level. This involves refusing to let ourselves concentrate on lusts until they entice and lure us into temptation (cf James 1:14-15). We can use the principle of replacement instead, and replace lustful thoughts with those that are pure and holy, as Paul recommended in Phillipians 4:8. We can rigorously school ourselves to forgive others whenever we feel even a hint of resentment beginning to grow. We can give of ourselves and our resources to help the sick and the poor and to spread the Good News. We can maintain our relationship with God through regular prayer, even when we don't think we have the time or the motivation. And we can pray, "Deliver us from the evil," knowing that our loving Daddy is even now doing just that.

The Closing Doxology

Most Christians have learned to close the model prayer with some variant of "For thine is the kingdom, the power, and the glory, Amen." Scholars universally acknowledge that these words do not appear in the earliest texts of the New Testament; they are a later addition. Most recent translations of the Bible omit them. These words do form a proper doxology for closing a formal prayer in the style of the ancient Jews and early Christians, and certainly express praise. But they do not seem to be a part of Jesus's original model prayer.

Other Forms of Prayer

Now that we have studied the Model Prayer, let's have a more general look at prayer.

> Once, in a certain place, Jesus was at prayer. When he ceased, one of his disciples said, "Lord, teach us to pray, as John taught his disciples." (Luke 11:1, NEB)

According to Luke, Jesus gave us the Lord's Prayer after the disciples had particularly noticed the Lord's own practice of prayer. Undoubtedly they had noticed not only that He prayed regularly, but He prayed with power and results. (Matthew places this event within the Sermon on the Mount. However, the book of Matthew is very carefully arranged into alternating sections of teaching and narrative. Many scholars believe that this arrangement was chosen because of the purpose for which Matthew wrote: to create a teaching text for new converts. Luke, on the other hand, describes his purpose in the first few verses of the book: to write a connected narrative about the words and work of Jesus. Thus Luke's account seems more likely to accurately describe the actual event.)

The literal question was, "How should we pray?" The implied question, coming as it did from good synagogue graduates, would have been, "How must we go beyond the traditions of Judaism in order to pray with the power and results that you do?" Jesus then answered with a model prayer that reinforced elements of traditional Jewish prayer, but that also added radical new elements. In order to understand the intent of the Lord's Prayer, though, we must see it in the context of Jewish prayer as a whole.

Characteristic forms of Jewish prayer included thanksgiving, praise, petition, intercession, and ritual prayer. These and other forms of prayer were adopted by the early church alongside the foundational prayer given us by the Lord himself.

Prayer of Thanksgiving

The need to offer thanksgiving is so basic to humanity that we should not need to talk much about it. Unfortunately, however, the desire to appear self-sufficient is so much a part of fallen humanity that we must emphasize thanksgiving as an antidote. We first find thanksgiving mentioned in the Bible in Leviticus 7. The wording there is interesting:

> This is the law of the peace offering which one may bring near unto Yahweh. If for thanksgiving he bring it near, then shall he bring near with the thanksgiving sacrifice perforated cakes, unleavened, overflowed with oil, and wafers unleavened, anointed with oil, and of fine flour moistened, perforated cakes overflowed with oil. (Leviticus 7:11-12, Rhm)

Notice that thanksgiving is not commanded; it is simply assumed! A person with any real relationship to God will at times feel overwhelmed with thanksgiving, and will need to express it. The ancient Hebrews only knew one way to thank God: sacrifice. Jesus has taught us much more about God. He taught us that we can speak our thanks, and that we can act out our thanks.

Jesus spoke His thanks to God on many occasions. At least four are given in the New Testament. He thanked God before distributing the food to the five thousand (Matthew 14:19) and the four thousand (Matthew 15:35). Matthew 11:10-27 and Luke 10:17-22 both tell of Jesus's surprising prayer in which He thanks God for having hidden the secret of miraculous power from the learned and wise, and revealing it to the simple. (Things haven't changed much in the last two thousand years. Many of today's learned and wise— by worldly standards— refuse to believe in God's ability or willingness to do miracles today, even though great numbers of those with simple faith find that God has not changed, nor is His arm shortened!) And John 11:41-44 tells us that Jesus publicly thanked God for hearing Him just before He raised Lazarus from the dead.

In many ways Jesus taught His followers of our oneness with Him, and therefore, of our oneness with each other. Examples are His final address given in John 14-17 and the story of the sheep and the goats in Matthew 25:31-40, both of which have been quoted earlier in this book. If we are one with Jesus, and He is one with God, then it follows that we can act out our thanks by doing for others what God has done for us. John puts it this way: "We love because he loved us first" (1 John 4:19 NEB), and again, "If God thus loved us, dear friends, we in turn are bound to love one another" (1 John 4:11, NEB). Since *agape* is love in action, we can act out our thanks to God by acting in love. In a sense, our actions performed with the purpose of honoring God are just as much prayer as the spoken word.

Many sermons have been preached on the subject of thankfulness. Often they direct us to be more thankful, but they seldom tell just how we are to do that. We cannot directly command ourselves to feel thankful, nor does it do any good for us to speak words of thanks to God when they are not in our hearts. But only a little reflection is needed for most of us to realize at least one thing for which we feel thankful. We can speak and act out our thankfulness for this one thing. As we do, other things often come to mind for which we want to thank God. Thankfulness is like a stream. If it is dammed up, it stops flowing. But when we break the dam by showing the humility to admit how grateful we are for even one thing, it starts flowing again.

Paul says: "In everything give thanks, for this [giving thanks] is a thing willed of God in Jesus Christ towards you." (1 Thessalonians 5:18, Rhm) This verse has been a sticking point for many Christians, because we often misread it. The initial Greek preposition *en* is correctly translated "in," but we often read it as "for". When an early Christian was being whipped for his faith, he was to give thanks, not for being whipped, but for whatever good God could bring out of the torturous experience. When the early translators of the Bible were being burned at the stake, they were to give thanks, not for the fire or the evil in the hearts of their persecutors, but that God could use this evil deed as a witness to His power in their lives. When we find ourselves in some sort of trouble, we are to give thanks, not for the trouble, but for the good that God can accomplish in our lives or the lives of others through it. This verse is properly understood when it is placed beside Romans 8:28: "We know further that unto them who love God, God causeth all things to work together for good." (Rhm)

I like to think of God as a master chess player. Seldom, if ever, can a chess player say that everything his opponent does is as he himself would have preferred. But a master chess player can take the moves that his opponent makes of his own free will and turn them to the master's advantage. God can turn the mistakes and the sins in our lives and the lives of our brothers and sisters into instruments for our growth. He can take sickness and disease that are brought on by our own mistakes and misunderstandings and those of our fellow fallen humans, and turn them to our benefit and His glory. He can take financial and emotional chaos in our lives and teach us to draw strength and understanding and compassion from it through which we can live better lives in the future. None of this means that evil is unreal, or that it is ever God's will.

As a teacher by profession, I sometimes found that a student would only settle down and engage the discipline to do homework after receiving a failing grade or two on a test. Some students have to flunk out of school because of their lack of discipline, and work at minimum wage for a few years, before seeing the importance of working toward a goal. I did not *choose* to "fail" these students, nor was I satisfied when some of them left college because of low grades. In no sense was the result of their actions— and non-actions!— my will. Yet I could be glad if later they learned from their experience. And they could be thankful when they came to their senses— not thankful that they failed, but thankful that they learned their lesson from the failure.

Of course there is a difference here. The student who has now succeeded can easily be thankful for the lesson learned through failure, because he has seen the lesson in his life. We are called upon to be thankful "in everything" even before we ever see the good that

God will bring out of evil. This demands faith, faith born of a personal relationship with God. Such a relationship demands a vital prayer life. When we have developed such a relationship, then we can sincerely say, "Daddy, I thank you for the good that I know you will bring out of this experience. Please help me stay aware of your presence and your love as I work to pass through the difficulty of this event, so that I may come out the other side of it having grown in my family resemblance to you."

At this point we remember that in Ephesians 5:20, Paul said, "... in the name of our Lord Jesus Christ give thanks every day for everything to our God and Father." (NEB) Here we are told to thank God *for* everything. As usual, we can get into trouble if we take pieces of the Bible out of context. The context of Ephesians 5:20 is an extended discourse on how Christians should live. It begins with chapter 4, verse 17: "This then is my word to you, and I urge it upon you in the Lord's name. Give up living like pagans... " (NEB) Paul discusses living in purity, speaking truth, not nursing anger, being honest, avoiding profane language, cultivating generosity, practicing forgiveness, shunning sexual sins, living in the light, and praising God. Then comes the word on thankfulness. We are to live in thankfulness to God. This does not mean that we are to thank God for evil things, or that evil is not real. It means that we are to cultivate a lifestyle that emphasizes and focuses on the things of God, and thanks Him for them. By giving no place to contemplation of evil, we minimize its effects on our lives.

Aileen was a model church secretary— dedicated, efficient, likeable. The professional staff and the congregation adored her. One bright November day she entered the church to begin work and was attacked, raped, and brutally murdered by an unknown assailant. Mary Alice and Dora were members of a church of the same denomination in a neighboring town. Neither of them had known Aileen, but both were naturally shocked by the newspaper accounts of the crime. There was no doubt in their minds that this evil deed had been inspired by the devil, and neither of them would have even considered that it could have been in any way the will of God. In her private prayers, Mary Alice thanked God that no such evil had befallen her and her friends, and prayed that the attacker might be brought to justice for the protection of the neighborhood. She also made doubly sure that her doors were locked at night. Dora reacted differently. She had additional locks installed on all her doors and retreated to their safety before sunset each day. In no event would she even walk to the curb to pick up a forgotten newspaper after dark. For months, most of her conversation was filled with the horror of Aileen's murder.

I think it is clear which of these two older women lived a thankful life, and which allowed the contemplation of evil to make her a prisoner of her own dread. This is exactly what Paul was talking about in Ephesians 5:20. He gives the same thought extra emphasis in Philippians.

> The Lord is near; have no anxiety, but in everything make your requests known to God in prayer and petition with thanksgiving. Then the peace of God, which is beyond our utmost understanding, will keep guard over your hearts and thoughts, in Jesus Christ.
> (Philippians 4:6-7, NEB)

How many things in our own lives do we face with anxiety? My own confession list would have to start with anxiety about what others think of me. I am anxious about what my students think, what my supervisor thinks, what the editor of this book thinks, what you, the reader, think, what my wife and kids think, etc., *ad infinitum.* What about you? Are you anxious about your money, your health, your family, or even your spiritual life? Paul reminds us that the Lord is near. If we have the faith to hear this word, its comfort should banish anxiety. But Paul gives us more help. We are to make our requests known to God with thanksgiving. Why should we do this? Surely God knows what we need before we ask Him. In fact, Jesus assured us that He does (Matthew 6:8b). It is by way of concession to our humanity that Paul gives this direction. It helps us to feel the presence of God if we verbalize our requests. As we will see later in this chapter, verbalizing our requests properly also gives us a new perspective on the things which make us anxious. And so does the other half of Paul's advice: offer prayer and petition *with thanksgiving!* What is to be the subject of the thanksgiving? First, we thank God because we recognize His continual care for us, as Mary Alice did. We also thank Him for answering our petitions. Yes, even before we see the answer manifested! Let's say you take your car to the service shop for a valve adjustment. You ask your regular mechanic if he has time to do the job today. He says yes, he'll get right on it. You do what? You thank him for helping you. Surely we can show as much faith in God as in our auto mechanic! But what if it's not God's will to answer as you have asked? More on this question later, but certainly we want to thank God for doing what is best for us, regardless of how His response compares with our request. Notice what Paul identifies as the outcome of bringing our requests and thanksgiving to God: peace!

> Gerald's daughter Caroline had learned to drive just three months before. Caroline was a bright girl, and generally very mature. But Gerald knew well the hazards that even an experienced driver faces, and he understood how much greater these dangers are for a new driver. Yet he also knew that part of releasing a teenager to become an adult in our society involves allowing her to drive on her own. For the first year, every time Caroline left with the family car, Gerald prayed specifically that God would keep her safe, surround her with protection, and help her to use good judgment. Gerald couldn't directly influence Caroline's safety on the highway any more than he had already done by careful instruction in defensive driving. But by turning over the situation to God in a prayer of faith, he could be sure that she was protected by Someone who loved her even more than he did, and who could keep her far safer than he ever could. Then he thanked God for protecting his daughter. In this he found peace.

Praise

> My God, my God, why hast thou forsaken me?
> Far from saving me

The words of my loud lamentation?
My God! I keep crying—
  By day and thou dost not answer, and
  By night and there is no rest for me.

But thou art holy,
  Who inhabitest the praises of Israel.

  In thee trusted our fathers,
They trusted, and thou didst deliver them;
  Unto thee made they outcry and escaped,
  In thee they trusted and had not turned pale.

But I am a worm and no one,
A reproach of men, and despised of a people;
All that see me laugh at me,
They open wide the mouth,
They shake the head:
  He should trust in Yahweh— let him deliver him—
  Let him rescue him seeing he delighteth in him.
For thou art he that severed me from the womb,
  He that caused me to trust upon the breasts of my mother;
  Upon thee was I cast from the time I was born,
  From the womb of my mother my God hast thou been.

Be not far from me for distress is near,
  For there is none to help.
Many bulls have surrounded me,
  Strong oxen of Bashan have enclosed me;
They have opened wide against me their mouth,
  A lion rending and roaring.

Like water I am poured out
And put out of joint are all my bones,
My heart hath become like wax,
It is melted in the midst of my body;

Dried as a potsherd is my strength,
And my tongue is made to cleave to my gums,
And in the dust of death wilt thou lay me.

For dogs have surrounded me,
An assembly of evil doers have encircled me,
They have pierced my hands and feet,
I may tell all my bones.
They look for— they behold me!
They part my garments among them,
And for my vestment they cast lots.

But thou O Yahweh be not far off,
Oh my help! to aid me make haste;
Rescue from the sword my life,
  From the power of the dog my solitary self:
Save me from the mouth of the lion,
Yea from the horns of the wild beasts hast thou
delivered me.

I will declare thy name unto my brethren,
In the midst of the convocation will I praise thee.

Ye that revere Yahweh praise him.
All ye the seed of Jacob glorify him,
And stand in awe of him all ye seed of Israel.
For he hath not despised nor abhorred the
humbling of the patient one,
Neither hath he hid his face from him,
But when he cried for help unto him he heard.

Of thee is my praise in the great convocation,
My vows will I pay before them who revere him.
The patient wronged-ones shall eat and be
satisfied.
They shall praise Yahweh who are seekers of
him,
  Let your heart live for aye.

All the ends of the earth will remember and turn
to Yahweh,
Yea all the families of the nations will bow
themselves down before thee,
For to Yahweh belongeth the kingdom,
And One to rule over the nations.
All the great ones of the earth shall eat and bow
down,
Before him shall kneel all that go down to the
dust,
Even he who had not kept alive his own soul!
My seed shall serve him,
It shall be recounted of the Lord to a generation
that shall come:
That his righteousness may be declared to a
people to be born,
   That he wrought with effect!
Psalm 22 (Rhm)

The Greek word for *praise* is not found in Jesus's mouth in the entire New Testament. However, as a child being brought up in the home of devoted Hebrew parents, He certainly went to the synagogue schools, where the course of study was the Scriptures. If you look at Jesus's words in a New Testament with cross-references, you will find that a great deal of what He said was taken directly from the Old Testament. Sometimes He quoted only a line of a familiar psalm, knowing that many of His listeners, also schooled in the synagogues, would call to mind the whole Scripture passage. I am convinced that this was His intention in quoting the first line of Psalm 22 when He was on the cross. But we miss the point if we concentrate only on the line He spoke. This was one of the mistakes made by the Docetic Gnostics in the second century. They believed that the Holy Spirit abandoned Jesus when He was on the cross, and that He was bemoaning that departure when He spoke of God forsaking Him. But if we look at the whole life of Jesus, we find that He *always* spoke and acted in faith, and often chastised the disciples for their lack of faith. Would He then show that same lack of faith Himself? I do not believe so.

Look at the rest of the psalm. Only two verses show the all-too-human reaction of despair. Then in verse 3, the psalm makes an extraordinary statement: "But thou art holy, who inhabitest the praises of Israel." God inhabits the praise of His people! Do you see the power in that revelation? Here is Jesus, hanging on the cross, awaiting what looks to all the world like the final triumph of His enemies. More than ever in His life, He needs to feel God's presence. What can He do to make that presence real to Himself? A line from a familiar psalm comes to His mind. In fact, it is a psalm that is in many ways prophetic of this very part of His mission. It says that God inhabits the praise of His people. Then after the prophecy of our Lord's suffering in verses 6 through 21, the rest of the psalm turns to praise.

Why did He not continue reciting the psalm? The physical position of a man being crucified is one of the most terrible parts of that torture. Not only was the Lord's body supported by nails driven through his wrists, but the natural sagging of the torso due to gravity caused pressure on the chest cavity. This made breathing very difficult. A victim of crucifixion had to periodically pull himself up against those excruciating nail wounds in order to get a decent breath. Talking was therefore doubly difficult. In addition to the constant pain, talking used more of the precious air, requiring more frequent exertion against the nails. Under these horrific conditions, did Jesus praise God from the cross? I believe He did. And I believe that His use of praise enabled Him to say, "It is accomplished," (John 19:30, NEB) and "Father, into thy hands I commit my spirit" (Luke 23:46, NEB).

Notice, by the way, that His last words are also from a psalm of faith and praise:

> Into thy hand do I commit my spirit
> Thou hast ransomed me Yahweh, God most faithful.
>
> I hate such as give heed to false vanities,
> I then in Yahweh have set my hope.

I will indeed exult and rejoice in thy
lovingkindness,
In that thou hast looked upon my humiliation,
Thou hast taken note that in distresses was my
life;
And hast not shut me up in the hand of the foe;
Thou hast given standing in a roomy place unto
my feet... .

Blessed be Yahweh,
　For he hath made wonderful his lovingkindness
for me, in a fortified city.

But I had said in mine alarm
　I am cut off from before thine eyes,
　But indeed thou didst hear the voice of my
supplication,
　When I cried for help unto thee.
Psalm 31:5-8, 21-22 (Rhm)

What then is the purpose of praise? Does God need to hear His
children say good things about Him, to bolster His ego? Doesn't the
very idea sound ridiculous? The purpose of praise is not that God
needs praise, but that *we need to praise Him.* In praise there is strength,
because praise puts us in a proper posture with respect to God. He is
(or should be) an example of everything we admire. When we remind
ourselves of His purity and love and kindness and strength, we
refocus ourselves on those very qualities. Then we can attune to Him
and feel His presence. And in praising God, we also develop some
humility, which most of us can use!

What then is the nature of praise? Early examples of praise in the
Scripture usually follow the example of Moses's song in Exodus 15:1-
18, which recounts God's mighty deeds on behalf of His people.
Miriam's song summarizes the content of Moses's song:

Sing to the LORD, for he has risen up in triumph;
the horse and his rider he has hurled into the sea.
Exodus 15:21 (NEB)

The Psalms echo this form of praise, but a new element is added: praise for God's intervention in the psalmist's personal life, as seen in the last six lines quoted above, from Psalm 31. It was probably praise modeled after this pattern that was spoken by people that Jesus and the apostles healed:

> He recovered his sight instantly and he followed Jesus, praising God. And all the people gave praise to God for what they had seen.
> Luke 18:43 (NEB)

> Then he [Peter] grasped him [the lame man] by the right hand and pulled him up; and at once his feet and ankles grew strong; he sprang up, stood on his feet, and started to walk. He entered the temple with them, leaping and praising God as he went.
> Acts 3:7-8 (NEB)

There were numerous examples of praise in the early church, and most of these echoed the Hebrew traditions of "praising by telling" of God's mighty works in the life of the church and of its individual members. The writer of Hebrews offers a new theological interpretation of praise:

> Our altar is one from which the priests of the sacred tent have no right to eat. As you know, those animals whose blood is brought as a sin-offering by the high priest into the sanctuary, have their bodies burned outside the camp, and therefore Jesus also suffered outside the gate, to consecrate the people by his own blood. Let us then go to him outside the camp, bearing the stigma that he bore. For here we have no permanent home, but we are seekers after the city which is to come. Through Jesus, then, let us continually offer up to God the sacrifice of praise, that is, the tribute of lips which

> acknowledge his name, and never forget to show
> kindness and to share what you have with others;
> for such are the sacrifices which God approves.
> Hebrews 13:10-16 (NEB)

The earlier sacrifices have been done away, since they could not purify, but only symbolize repentance. Jesus has given Himself as the sacrifice that does purify— not that God required a sacrifice, but that the nature of our sin is such that we did. Therefore, our natural response, approved by God, is to praise Him by acknowledging His Name, and to help our brothers and sisters. What does it mean to acknowledge His Name? We have already discussed that the Name means that God is One, and that He is the only God. We also have emphasized that He is good, that He is Love, that He is our Daddy, and that Jesus represents all of God that can be expressed in human form. When we acknowledge these things, we acknowledge His Name, and we praise in the way that God approves.

Petition

Who am I to be telling God what to do? This is a very legitimate question asked by many rational people. The question, of course, answers itself. The creature does not tell the Creator how to run His creation. Or in Paul's imagery (Romans 9:21), the pot does not protest to the potter. Why, then, do we make prayers of petition?

Stop for a moment and think about how far we've come in this book. One of our early concerns was to discover just what prayer is, and we found that "prayer" is not a very good word for it, because in English *prayer* means "request". Because of this confusion, too many people think prayer is only, or at least primarily, requesting. Now we are raising the question whether the requesting is a function of prayer at all! But doesn't this question answer itself also? Can we imagine fellowship with an earthly parent in which we do not at some time make requests?

So we have a paradox. Too often when we are confronted by a paradox we give up on finding the truth. This is the lazy way out. Whenever we find a paradox— a seeming contradiction— in spiritual studies, we have found a challenge to a new level of understanding.

And so it is here. The key to this new level is to recognize the way in which God has chosen to exercise His power in the earth. God has given us free will and has limited Himself so that He will not violate that free will. The New Testament identification of the Church as the body of Christ is much more deeply true than we usually suppose. In fact, God has chosen to act through us, individually and collectively, to bring His kingdom to reality. Therefore, for Him to act supernaturally to heal a problem, one or more people must invite His help. In John's vision, Jesus said, "Here I stand knocking at the door; if anyone hears my voice and opens the door, I will come in and sit down to supper with him and he with me." (Revelation 3:20, NEB) He knocks because He will not be the unbidden guest. He will not override our free will.

So we make prayers of petition to invite God to intervene in our world. Does it follow that God always will do what we ask? It depends upon what we ask. And no, this is not to evade the question, but to bring us to a crucial point in understanding prayers of petition. Let us read some Scripture:

> Indeed anything you ask in my name I will do it,
> so that the Father may be glorified in the Son.
> (John 14:13, NEB)

> If you dwell in me, and my words dwell in you,
> ask what you will, and you shall have it.
> (John 15:7, NEB)

> You do not get what you want, because you do not pray for it. Or, if you do, your requests are not granted because you pray from wrong motives, to spend what you get on your pleasures.
> (James 4:2-3, NEB)

> Dear friends, if our conscience does not condemn us, then we can approach God with confidence, and obtain from him whatever we

> ask, because we are keeping his commands and
> doing what he approves.
> (1 John 3:21-22, NEB)

> We can approach God with confidence for this
> reason: if we make requests which accord with
> his will he listens to us; and if we know that our
> requests are heard, we also know that the things
> we ask for are ours.
> (1 John 4:14-16, NEB)

Notice that all these scriptures say the same thing: we will receive what we ask for in our prayers if we ask according to God's will. This places upon us the burden of knowing what is God's will before we pray. This would be an impossible test if we hadn't already been given the answers. But we have! The principles of God's will are outlined in the Bible, and if we study it as a whole, we will find wisdom to know the will of God for most situations. The key word here is *study.* Just reading the Bible is not enough. We must stay alert as we read, even when the words are familiar. Often reading in several translations helps. And we must meditate on what we have read.

Christian meditation is not to be confused with Transcendental Meditation, although the two have some things in common. The purpose of Christian meditation is to listen to God, to open our minds to what He will say to us, and to make ourselves available to Him for His work. Most other forms of meditation emphasize emptying the mind. Christian meditation has been called "practicing the Presence," because it involves emptying the mind of hindrances and worries in order to fill it with the consciousness of God's presence. If you need to learn more about Christian meditation, there are many excellent books; some of the best include:

> *A Spiritual Formation Workbook*, by James Bryan Smith
> *Meditating on the Word*, by Dietrich Bonhoeffer.
> *Meditation and the Mind of Man*, by Herbert Bruce Puryear
> *Discovering the Depths*, by William Clemmons
> *Celebration of Discipline*, by Richard J. Foster

The Practice of His Presence, by Laubach and Lawrence
The Cloud of Unknowing, edited by Richard Johnston

Works by Richard Rolle, St. John of the Cross, and Julian of Norwich are also excellent. (You should be aware, though, that except for the first six, these authors reflect a strong medieval perspective such that practical application for modern folk requires careful interpretation.)

Since none of us is perfect, there will always be areas in which our understanding is incomplete, even after we have studied the Scripture and meditated. But of course there is no penalty for praying out of line with God's will, except that the prayer will not be answered in the way we had hoped.

There are two equally mistaken lines of thought about prayer. One says, "The Bible says I can have whatever I pray for. It's a blank check."

This statement ignores the crucial "if" clause that is stated or implied in each of the scriptures above: *if* we pray in line with God's will. The other erroneous idea is, "You never can tell when God is going to answer a prayer... it may not be His will to answer... so you just hope and pray." This is wrong because it completely lacks faith. The writer of Hebrews says that without faith it is impossible to please God (11:6), and James tells us that he who prays must "ask in faith, without a doubt in his mind; for the doubter is like a heaving sea ruffled by the wind. A man of that kind must not expect the Lord to give him anything; he is double-minded, and can never keep a steady course." (1:6-8, NEB) So before we pray, we need to make sure that we are praying in line with God's will. If for some reason we are unsure of that, James instructs us: "If any of you falls short in wisdom, he should ask God for it and it will be given him, for God is a generous giver who neither refuses nor reproaches anyone." (James 1:5, NEB)

Raphael had worked as an accountant for a large multinational corporation for six years. During that time, he had become convinced that he did not want to spend the rest of his working life with a company of that kind. The environment not only seemed to encourage laziness, it almost required it. Periodically there would not be enough work to do, and Raphael's job was not one that put him in the position of being able to find work if it was not assigned to him. Thus he had many days in which he simply had to look busy. Finally, Raphael decided to resign and go into business for himself. He did so with all the assurance of youth, and without asking for God's guidance in the matter. During the predictable hard times that most young businesses must endure, Raphael and his wife often prayed for God to help them succeed in their business. Nevertheless, several years later, the business was forced to close. After a year without steady work, Raphael was offered a job teaching accounting. He had never considered teaching as a career option, but needed the income, so he accepted. Very soon, he realized that he enjoyed work more, and was more fulfilled by it, than ever before in his life. Many years later, he realized that God had been working in his life all along. His real desire was for a job that used his skills and brought satisfaction. He prayed in accordance with his own limited opinion of what such a job would be. God answered his prayer in a way that was far better than Raphael's own life-design would have permitted. But it was not the way Raphael had envisioned.

If Raphael had taken time to study and pray and meditate concerning God's will for his life, he probably would not have taken the job with the large corporation in the first place. Even if he had, he would not likely have subsequently started his own business. He could have entered teaching directly, and avoided much grief. And he would not have had the severe testing of his faith that resulted from constantly praying— in vain, it seemed— for the success of his business, which Raphael saw in retrospect was not a part of God's will for his life. In fact, at the time he was running his business, Raphael could have prayed much more effectively by asking (and trusting) God to do whatever was best for him at that point in his life. This sort of open-ended prayer does not attempt to limit God by specifying how He should answer, but trusts Him to do the best. It is a prayer of faith— not faith in the process of prayer, but faith in the person of God. Any time we decide exactly what we need for God to do, and then tell

Him just what that is, we had better be sure that our decision has been guided by God rather than self! Whenever we are not sure of the will of God in a certain situation, an open prayer may be our best approach, because then we can focus our faith on God's loving judgment as to what is best for us.

Let me point out something that seems painfully obvious. No prayer we can pray will change God, or change His mind. Yet how often do we pray as though we had to persuade God to change to our way of thinking? Our task— before the prayer begins— is to change our way of thinking to conform to God's way. Once we have done that, the prayer of petition will often be much changed, and may even be unnecessary. Prayer is not telling God what to do, but rather inviting the Spirit of God to flow through us. He stands at the door and knocks, and we must invite Him in; He will not be a celestial errand-boy to go and do our bidding. The prayer of petition involves a spirit of, "Come, Lord, and I will do your bidding," not the reverse. This explains the seeming illogic of our having to pray for God to do His own will. In prayer, we are answering the knock at the door; we are inviting Him to act in a specific situation in a way that He would not do without our permission, because it would violate our free will, or nullify it by interfering with the law of cause and effect.

In our prayer then, how do we make our requests in such a way that we conform to that will? We have just seen that the first principle is that our motives must be right. This does not mean that we are not to pray for things for ourselves, but that since our whole lives are supposed to be involved with helping others, anything for ourselves that we pray for is to be something that will help us to help others. We can count on results when we pray for wisdom in dealing with a thorny interpersonal situation, but a prayer for a new set of golf clubs is less likely to be answered favorably. The motive for the first prayer would be helping, while that for the second is purely personal pleasure. Does this say that God is opposed to pleasure? No, of course not. He has given us the ability to earn the money to buy things for our pleasure. In fact, He commanded the Hebrews to use their tithes for holy partying, as a celebration of thanksgiving! (Deuteronomy 14:22-28) But what do you think would be the result if God were to supernaturally supply everything we desired for our pleasure? I doubt if any human could avoid dissolution; I certainly don't think I could.

The second principle is that our petitions are not to be in the nature of informing God of our needs. "Your Father knows what your needs are before you ask him." (Matthew 6:8b, NEB) Let us say that you have had a problem with your finances for several years. Each day you have prayed for money enough to meet your expenses. You are not thinking about golf clubs, but the rent. Yet the problem remains. There are many possible reasons: lack of faith, failure to tithe on what you do have, and so on. But all of these can be lumped into a need to learn a lesson. Life is about learning. Even our Lord "learned obedience in the school of suffering, and, once perfected, became the source of eternal salvation for all who obey him." (Hebrews 5:8-9, NEB) When we have a persistent problem, that means we have not learned the lesson that will free us from it. As long as we pray daily for money to ease our financial problems, we betray in ourselves a belief that money is the answer to our problem. In fact, it is not. God can use money, along with other means, to eliminate our financial problems, but He is not restricted to any one solution. If we pray sincerely for understanding of our real problem, then act on the understanding that comes, our financial problem will be removed. Notice that I did not say that we would receive more money. We may. We may find a way to spend less on what we need. We may find that our values change so that our perception of our needs changes. But the problem will be removed when we have learned its lesson.

> Therefore I bid you to put away anxious thoughts about food and drink to keep you alive, and clothes to cover your body. Surely life is more than food, the body more than clothes. Look at the birds of the air; they do not sow and reap and store in barns, yet your heavenly Father feeds them. You are worth more than the birds! Is there a man of you who by anxious thought can add a foot to his height? And why be anxious about clothes? Consider how the lilies grow in the fields; they do not work, they do not spin;

and yet, I tell you, even Solomon in all his
splendour was not attired like one of these. But if
that is how God clothes the grass in the fields,
which is there today and tomorrow is thrown on
the stove, will he not all the more clothe you?
How little faith you have! No, do not ask
anxiously, "What are we to eat? What are we to
drink? What shall we wear?" All these are things
for the heathen to run after, not for you, because
your heavenly Father knows that you need them
all. Set your minds on God's kingdom and his
justice before everything else, and all the rest will
come to you as well.
(Matthew 6:25-33, NEB)

The prayers of petition in the New Testament are very consistent
with these instructions. Many of these prayers will be discussed under
the heading, "Intercessory Prayer."

In the two non-intercessory prayers whose content we glimpse, Jesus
prayed for help in achieving His mission. Luke 6:12-16 tells us that
Jesus spent the night in prayer before He called the Twelve from
among His disciples. It is reasonable to assume that He was praying
for guidance. And in the final hours before the crucifixion, Matthew
26, Mark 14, and Luke 22 all tell us of our Lord's only recorded
prayer for Himself: "My Father, if it is possible, let this cup pass me
by. Yet not as I will, but as thou wilt." (Matthew 26:39b, NEB) Son
of God in a unique way that passes our understanding, yet Son of
Man also, He called to His loving Father out of a heart "ready to
break with grief," asking to be spared the horror that was to come.
Yet even in this time, He placed His mission first, asking above all
that God's will be done. Had He not added that last line, the
crucifixion would not have occurred, because Jesus told Peter only
minutes later that if He appealed to His Father, He would at once
send more than twelve legions of angels— but then the scriptures
would not be fulfilled. And yet there is a sense in which even this
prayer of Jesus was not for Himself. Notice that, at Gethsemane, He
took Peter, James, and John with Him and told them to watch and
pray. When they fell asleep, He awakened them and repeated the

prayer twice. Still they fell asleep. And yet we have the account of what He prayed. So after the resurrection, Jesus must have told at least some of the disciples what He prayed on that dark night in Gethsemane. Was He setting an example for us? When we are almost overcome with horror and grief— notice that fear was not mentioned!— our Father understands our prayer for relief, even though we may not be sure that the prayer is in line with God's will. But we must still remember Whose we are and Whose work we are to be about, and yield the final decision to Him.

At several times in His ministry, Jesus told the disciples specific things to pray for. In Matthew 9:38 they were told to "beg the owner to send labourers to harvest his crop." (NEB) They were to pray for physical assistance at the time of the destruction of Jerusalem (which took place in AD 66): "Pray that it may not be in winter when you have to make your escape, or Sabbath." (Matthew 24:20, NEB) "Be on the alert, praying at all times for strength to pass safely through all these imminent troubles and to stand in the presence of the Son of Man." (Luke 21:36, NEB) And they were adjured to "stay awake, and pray that you may be spared the test." (Matthew 26:41b, NEB) Notice that none of these prayers is in any sense self-gratifying; they are all directed toward the goal to which He has called us.

One other personal petition is specifically recommended by Scripture in James 5:13: "Is any of you in trouble? He should turn to prayer." (NEB) This is really very general. We can be in trouble in many ways, and often are! Although at their root, most of our troubles are spiritual, they manifest as physical, mental, emotional, financial, and social troubles. We may need wisdom, strength, vision, or even physical or financial help. If we have made a practice of studying the Scriptures, we will usually have a good idea of how to pray for help in our troubled times. But if we have not, or if we find it difficult to understand or apply what we have studied to our present problem, the following sections may help.

What Do We Seek to Change?

> In your prayers do not go babbling on like the
> heathen, who imagine that the more they say the
> more likely they are to be heard. Do not imitate
> them.
> Matthew 6:7-8a (NEB)

ow often have you heard these two phrases in public prayers:
H"Lord, give us peace," or "Lord, be with us"? Both of these, and
several other "prayer-talk" formulae qualify as "babbling on like the
heathen." Why? What's wrong with them? Surely there's nothing
wrong with the desires they express. But they request favors that
have already been granted. In John 14:27, Jesus tells the disciples:
"Peace is my parting gift to you, my own peace, such as the world
cannot give. Set your troubled hearts at rest, and banish your fears"
(NEB). In John 17:20-21, Christ made it clear that He was addressing
His disciples for all time, not just the ones in the room, when He
said: "But it is not for these alone that I pray, but for those also who
through their words put their faith in me; may they all be one: as
thou, Father, art in me, and I in thee, so also may they be in us, that
the world may believe that thou didst send me." (NEB) If therefore
Jesus has already given us peace, does it make sense to continue
asking Him for peace?

> The eleven disciples made their way to Galilee, to
> the mountain where Jesus had told them to meet
> him. When they saw him, they fell prostrate
> before him, though some were doubtful. Jesus
> then came up and spoke to them. He said: "Full
> authority in heaven and on earth has been
> committed to me. Go forth therefore and make
> all nations my disciples; baptize men everywhere
> in the name of the Father and the Son and the
> Holy Spirit, and teach them to observe all that I
> have commanded you. And be assured, I am with
> you always, to the end of time."
> Matthew 28:16-20 (NEB)

Surely no Christian believes that the Great Commission was given just to the Eleven. We know that it applies to us also. In that case, He has also promised us that He is with us always. So why ask Him to be with us?

The underlying principle here is not that we somehow offend God by asking in vain, but that our prayers are hindered by our using mindless formulae whose very wording implies that by our prayers we can somehow change God's mind. The problem, my friends, is within us. If we do not experience God's peace, it is because we allow the cares of the world and the false glamour of wealth to enter in and choke the Word. (See Matthew 13:22.) It is certainly appropriate to pray for wisdom and understanding concerning our failure to experience peace. If, however, we are serious about this request, we will also "seek peace and pursue it" through Bible study, meditation, and the study of books and articles written by other people who are traveling the spiritual path. Sincere prayers for help in realigning our values to accord with God's values are always fruitful. The same things can be said for the times when we don't feel God's presence. Given: Yahweh is a God of truth. Given: He said (through His Son) that He is always with us. Given: We are not yet perfect. Given: We sometimes do not feel His presence. Now where is the problem: with God, or with us? And how do we pray sensibly for help in overcoming it? This answers itself, once we throw away the "prayer-talk" traditions of men and look intelligently at the situation.

When Do We Need to Say "Thy Will Be Done"?
The phrase "Thy will be done" comes from the mouth of Jesus twice in the New Testament. The first time is when He gives us the Lord's Prayer. We are to pray that in general God's will shall be done. We are to align our desires with His will. The second time is in Gethsemane, when Jesus prays that this cup may pass Him by without His drinking it. His heart almost breaking with grief, Jesus wants to stay with the disciples and help them to grow past the immense lack of understanding that He has just seen in them. (Read John 14-17 to get a feel for just how poorly they understood the Lord's mission on the very night before the crucifixion.) Yet He senses that this prayer may not be in line with the will of God. So He

specifically amends His prayer to emphasize the priority of God's will.

Likewise, when we make a specific request of God that we are not sure is in line with His will, we are to follow Jesus's example. First, we are to have the faith and humility to honestly prefer God's will to our own. (This is not so hard to do if we realize Who He is!) Secondly, we then express that faith and humility by affirming our desire for God's will to prevail.

> Tim approached the new bicycle with all the eager assurance of a five-year-old. "Daddy, let me ride it! Turn loose and let me do it! You and Mama gave it to me!"
>
> "But Tim, there's a big difference between this and your tricycle. You have to… "
>
> "I can do it, Daddy. Let me try."

We smile at this picture of the simple courage of youth pitted against the cautious concern of maturity. And yet how many times do we go to God with our own cry of "Daddy, let me do it!" without first searching for guidance or confirmation or preparation for whatever "it" is? If Tim persuades his daddy to let him try the bicycle without any instruction, we hope inwardly that the inevitable falls will not hurt too much. Our Daddy will not violate our free will, and just as Jesus said that God would send angels to free Him from the Jews, God may even grant our requests that do not accord with His best will for us. "Nevertheless, Thy will be done" is not a capitulation to second-best, as it feels to our egos, but acknowledgment that the best may be better than we could ask or think, and that God wills the best for us in every situation.

There is, however, a "however"! "Nevertheless, Thy will be done" is not to be used as a crutch for our failure to try to learn God's will for us. When we use the phrase in this way, it becomes very difficult to pray with faith. Faith comes most easily when we are sure that we want what God wants. This assurance comes by prayer and meditation and Bible study.

How about mistakes? Yes, we all misinterpret God's will. Many years ago I asked God to interpret all my prayers as requests, not just for the specific things that I mentioned, but as requests that He act for the best in my life in whatever areas I was praying about. I can now petition my Daddy with the knowledge that:

> ... if we make requests which accord with his will, he listens to us; and if we know that our requests are heard, we also know that the things we ask for are ours.
> (I John 5:14b-15, NEB)

How Do Prayers of Petition Work?

The book of James tells us that, "A good man's prayer is powerful and effective." (James 5:16b, NEB) Yet there are many times that each of us has prayed and not been able to see that the prayer was effective at all. It's enough to make us wonder just what it takes to qualify as a "good man". [The Greek is *dikaiou*, meaning "righteous". There is no noun (*man*). The word is used to mean "righteous one" or "just one", much as in the phrase, "The just shall live by faith" (Hebrews 10:38, KJV)]. Thus the Greek is gender-inclusive, so we could as well say, "The just person shall live by faith." In fact, we are made righteous or just by faith:

> Therefore, now that we have been justified through faith, let us continue at peace with God through our Lord Jesus Christ, through whom we have been allowed to enter the sphere of God's grace, where we now stand.
> (Romans 5:1-2a, NEB)

> Christ was innocent of sin, yet for our sake God made him one with the sinfulness of men, so that in him we might be made one with the goodness of God himself.
> (2 Corinthians 5:21, NEB)

So it does not matter how we feel about our standing with God. We qualify as "good persons". And because of this very goodness that is a part of our salvation, we fight against the corners of evil in ourselves, and we repent of the sins that we do commit. We only need to believe that we are truly justified in God's eyes.

But still, some people's prayers seem to be more successful than others'. The difference is not in how much "pull" a given person has with God, because "...God has no favourites... " (Acts 10:34b, NEB). The difference is in how we pray. The centrality of faith has already been mentioned, as has the need to pray in line with God's will, and the discipline required to do that. In order to understand the next step in effective prayer, we need to understand something of how prayer petitions work. In addition to permitting God to work in our lives, our prayer petitions allow us to speak to our own negative thought- and habit-patterns. In the last century and a half, we have discovered much about the operation of the human subconscious mind. The American psychologist William James described this hidden portion of the human mind in the late 1800's. Dr. Thomas Jay Hudson called it "the subjective mind". Sigmund Freud coined the term *unconscious* and devoted a great deal of study to it, as did his best-known pupil, Carl Gustav Jung. They all agreed that this subliminal part of the mind controls the involuntary actions of the body, such as heartbeat, digestion, and so on, and that the subliminal mind is incapable of inductive logic. However, it will respond to suggestions, correctly deduce their logical results, and act upon them, provided that these are in accord with the basic principles of right and wrong accepted by the conscious mind, and also provided that the suggestions do not involve serious danger to the person's body. So-called post-hypnotic suggestions act through the subliminal mind, as do the feats of yoga masters, who have demonstrated in scientific tests that they can "turn off" pain in their bodies, cause almost immediate healing of wounds, and go into states resembling suspended animation.[2] More recently, psychologists using biofeedback techniques have been able to duplicate these feats without the years of training that the yogis had to endure. Dr. Stanley Krippner and others at Saybrook and Stanford Universities have

---

[2]Elmer Green and Alyce Green, *Beyond Biofeedback* (New York: Delacorte, 1977).

demonstrated the ability of most people to transmit and receive telepathic messages[3, 4]. (Actually, hypnotherapists learned this fact much earlier, as many subjects were clearly able to pick up on what the therapist was thinking.) All these threads point to a significant part of the working of prayer: if you or I offer a prayer in faith, it acts as a suggestion to our own subconscious minds, which we are then likely to act upon. Prayers for other people can be perceived telepathically by those other people without their even being aware of it, and can affect them in the same way.

At this point, you may be thinking, "Just a minute, here. So far, this book has been good, sound Christianity. Why are we all of a sudden oozing into psychology or New Age stuff or whatever this is?"

Let me make three comments. First, Jesus summarized His mission to Pilate by saying that He had come to bear witness to the truth. We are therefore bound to embrace the truth wherever we find it. The Roman Catholic Church refused to accept the truth of the Copernican view of the universe, even after it had been proven to be a more accurate description than the Ptolemaic one (which, by the way, was Greek in its origin, not Christian). They refused because they were bound by their own limited perceptions, and thought that these perceptions were God's truth. We like to identify with Copernicus and Galileo, but I suspect that most of us have a great deal more in common with that sixteenth-century pope and his cardinals when it comes to confusing our habitual opinions with The Truth.

Second, not only is this explanation of a part of the working of prayer scientifically valid, but it explains a fact well-known to any serious student of prayer in a variety of religions: that Hindus and Buddhists and Shintoists and even voodoo-worshippers can often

---

[3]Montague Ullman, Stanley Krippner, and Alan Vaughan, *Dream Telepathy: Experiments in Nocturnal ESP* (New York:Macmillan 1974).

[4]Russel Targ and Harold Puthoff, *Mind Reach* (New York: Delacorte, 1977).

give examples of having prayers answered.[5] When the sick came to Jesus for healing, He almost always said, "Your faith has made you whole." Notice that He never said, "Your faith in Me has made you whole." At the time of their healing, many of those who were healed knew nothing about Jesus except that He could heal them. They certainly were not believers in Jesus's divinity or His resurrection (which had not happened yet). The paralyzed man whose healing is described in John 5 did not even know who Jesus was when the healing took place. The strong faith of these people, called into being by the power of God working through Jesus Himself, healed them.

Third, please note that I have not said anywhere that God is not involved in answering prayers, only that the phenomenon of suggestion is also involved. Undeniably, some prayers are answered in ways that are explainable only by divine intervention. Certainly God hears all our prayers, and acts directly sometimes. But I believe that He also lets us answer our own prayers, and sometimes those of our brothers and sisters, too. Think of this example. If your child came up to you and asked for a dollar to buy some ice cream, then in the process of asking realized that the money was already in his or her pocket, would it detract from your loving, providing nature as a parent for you to let the child use that money to make the purchase? Or if two children were playing together and one asked you where her toy shovel was, would it be disrespectful to you if the other child noticed it close by and handed it to her? All of us humans are brothers and sisters in a deeper way than we usually imagine. And Jesus was not speaking figuratively when He said that all Christians are one. Why, then, should we object to the idea that we are subconsciously aware of another's prayer for us?

The reason for spending so much time on this idea is that it helps us to understand the need for faith. If a hypnotherapist says to a patient, "Now try to relax," it is unlikely that relaxation will occur. Using the word *try* implies a possibility of failure, and doubt causes the

---

[5]For an enlightening discussion of current scientific research on the power of healing prayer, see *Healing Words*, by Larry Dossey, M. D. (San Francisco: Harper-Collins, 1993).

suggestion to be ineffective. But if the therapist says, "Now you can feel yourself becoming more relaxed and peaceful, like the smooth, calm surface of a pond," the suggestion will usually produce the intended result. In the same way, if we pray, "God, if it is possible, help me to become less timid when I speak in public," our prayer's effect on our own subconscious is less effective than if we say, "Please help me to see myself as a fine public speaker, filled with vibrant self-confidence." If we then focus for a few minutes on the image of ourselves standing before a rapt crowd, speaking dynamically, then our faith is reinforced. If we follow this by thanking our Father for answering our prayer, and then put the matter out of our minds, we will truly have offered a prayer in faith.

Now we can also see more clearly the importance of praying in line with God's will. If we have taken the time to discover His will before we pray, our confidence is greatly enhanced when we do pray.

Try as we might, however, our consciousness is limited, and our understanding is limited. We see through a poor mirror, rather than face to face. So we will sometimes (perhaps often!) pray for something that is not best for us, or maybe not even what we really want. This is the reason that:

> ...the Spirit comes to the aid of our weakness.
> We do not even know how we ought to pray, but
> through our inarticulate groans the Spirit himself
> is pleading for us, and God who searches our
> inmost being knows what the Spirit means,
> because he pleads for God's people in God's
> own way; and in everything, as we know, he co-
> operates for good with those who love God and
> are called according to his purpose.
> (Romans 8:26-28, NEB)

Often sermons have painted the picture of the Spirit on His knees before the Father, pleading and begging for us. I think this is a mistake. The Greek word *hyperentynchanei* means "to intercede for," so the word *plead* is used in a legal sense. I believe that the idea of the Spirit as interpreter is more enlightening. Paul is not saying that our

Father cannot understand us, but just the opposite. He can, and does understand us perfectly, through the ministry of that part of God that we call the Spirit. This is the whole point. And because God understands us so perfectly, we can come before Him with all the more confidence!

One other serious concern many people have is whether God will break into the cycle of cause and effect to deliver us from the results of our own errors. Sure, we're forgiven, but will that fact alter our physical circumstances that have been damaged by our sin? Cause and effect is the Law of the universe.

The Law given in the Pentateuch codifies the concept of this Great Law. The Hebrews were right: the Law is an image of God. Creation occurred through the Law.

In *The Lion, the Witch, and the Wardrobe*, there is a scene that helps us understand this point. In this book, Aslan the lion is the Christ figure, the talking animals are on his side in the conflict, and Lucy, Peter, Susan, and Edmund represent humankind. Edmund has knowingly betrayed his brother and sisters, as well as Aslan and the animals. The witch has just requested a meeting with Aslan. There she demands the blood of the "human creature" Edmund, since the Emperor-Over-Sea's "Deep Magic" gives her the right to a kill for every treachery committed.

> "Come and take it then," said the Bull with the man's head in a great bellowing voice.
>
> "Fool," said the Witch with a savage smile that was almost a snarl, "do you really think your master can rob me of my rights by mere force? He knows the Deep Magic better than that. He knows that unless I have blood as the Law says all Narnia will be overturned and perish in fire and water."
>
> "It is very true," said Aslan; "I do not deny it."

"Oh, Aslan!" whispered Susan in the Lion's ear, "can't we—I mean, you won't, will you? Can't we do something about the Deep Magic? Isn't there something you can work against it?"

"Work against the Emperor's magic?" said Aslan turning to her with something like a frown on his face. And nobody ever made that suggestion to him again.[6]

As the scene continues, Aslan secures an agreement with the Witch through which his own life is given in place of Edmund's. But our point is that the Law is not merely the legislation of God; it is a revelation of His character. Therefore, Aslan will not work against the Emperor's Deep Magic: God— Father, Son, or Holy Spirit— will not violate His own Law. But a greater cause can intervene between a lesser cause and its effect. Paul says:

> But death held sway from Adam to Moses, even over those who had not sinned as Adam did, by disobeying a direct command— and Adam foreshadows the Man who was to come. But God's grace is out of all proportion to Adam's wrongdoing... where sin was... multiplied, grace immeasurably exceeded it, in order that, as sin established its reign by way of death, so God's grace might establish its reign in righteousness, and issue in eternal life through Jesus Christ our Lord.
> (Romans 5:14-15a, 20b-21 NEB)

Christ's sacrificial life and death and resurrection constituted a greater cause that intervenes between that other cause— human sin— and its effect— death. In the same way, God is able to act in the much smaller causes and effects of our daily lives to bring good even out of our errors. The Law was sent as a kind of tutor. (See Galatians 3:24.) When we have learned a part of the lesson, the tutor does not need to continue hammering us with that part. At the same time, physical

---

[6]C. S. Lewis, *The Lion, the Witch, and the Wardrobe* (New York: Macmillan, 1950), 137-140.

actions have physical consequences, and if God were to deliver us from every consequence of our errors, He would be robbing us of the reality of our free will. This He will not do. Our conclusion must be, then, that God is a God of grace, and we can count fully on that grace, even though sometimes (not always!) it must be a tough grace that allows us to experience the effects of our sins.

Prayer of Intercession

Most of the great prayers in both the Old and New Testaments are prayers for others, prayers of intercession. Abraham asked God to spare Sodom and Gomorrah if ten good men could be found there (Genesis 18:23-33). Moses prayed that God would spare the idolatrous Hebrews after they had made the golden calf at Mount Sinai (Exodus 2:11-14). Jesus prayed for the children (Matthew 19:13); He prayed that Simon Peter's faith would not fail (Luke 22:32); He prayed for God to send the Holy Spirit to comfort the disciples (John 14:16); He prayed for protection and unity for the disciples (John 17:9-26). Jesus gave instructions to pray for our persecutors (Matthew 5:44) and for laborers in God's harvest (Matthew 9:38). The church prayed for Peter's safety (Acts 12:5). Paul prayed for growth of love and discernment among the believers (Phillipians 1:9), for forgiveness of Alexander the copper-smith, and for salvation of the Jews (Romans 10:1). James instructs the congregations to pray for the sick and to pray for one another in general (James 5:14-16). John tells us to pray for each other's forgiveness (I John 5:16), and he himself prays for the health and prosperity of Gaius (III John 1:2). We are told that the first deacons were elected so that the Twelve could devote themselves to prayer and ministry of the word (Acts 6:4). Clearly prayer of intercession is of very great importance.

Many people, though, have problems understanding intercessory prayer. They say, "Why should I have to ask God to help someone whom He loves just as much as He loves me?" Certainly if we view intercession as trying to persuade God to do something nice for some other person or group, this objection is valid. But we have already seen that prayer is first choosing to relate to God. As we do that consistently, we become more like God. He cares; we come to care. As we pray sincerely for others, we ourselves grow. And when we pray for others, we become more likely to do for them what we can at the physical, material, and emotional levels. We have also seen that prayer can act directly in the life of another person, helping to bring peace, guidance, mental clarity, or healing. Experiments have shown conclusively that prayer can directly enhance or retard the growth of bacteria and fungi.[7] Cases of telepathic contact between twins are well-known. There is growing evidence that telepathic contact between humans at the subconscious level is the rule rather than the exception. It appears that God has designed us with the ability to minister directly to each other through intercessory prayer. Many of us have been taught in church that we are "Jesus's hands and feet". Perhaps this is truer than we knew. Perhaps our prayer of intercession is important because we can directly help others just by praying. An important part of the action of praying for another is simply that doing so is a way of expressing love for that person.

A corollary of the action of intercessory prayer through direct telepathy is the need to be very careful not to pray for someone against that person's will.

> Marianne's son Rob was in the midst of teenage rebellion. Knowing that it is common for children of Rob's age to buck against their parents' ideas did not help Marianne. Nor did Marianne's tendency to speak her mind on any and all occasions help Rob at this point in his life. As a result, Marianne often felt frustrated, worried, and unappreciated. Rob felt angry and confused. Finally, Marianne decided that to keep peace in the house, she had better try her best to soft-pedal her suggestions to Rob, and to give him freedom to make all the decisions that he could handle. At first, the idea worked. Rob's behavior and attitude improved, and he seemed to feel less need to rebel. But soon the bottling-up

---

[7] J. Barry, "General and Comparative Study of the Psychokinetic Effect on a Fungus Culture," *Journal of Parapsychology* 32 (1968): 237-243.

C. B. Nash, "Psychokinetic Control of Bacterial Growth," *Journal of the American Society for Psychical Research* 51 (1982): 217-221.

effort became overwhelming to Marianne. Her best friend Hazel suggested that she use intercessory prayer to deal with her need to guide Rob. So she began doing just that. The first prayer session lasted for almost an hour, as she unburdened herself of all that she wanted God to do for Rob. She prayed for God to guide, protect, lead, push, cajole, needle, and prompt her son. But when the prayer was finished, she was even more upset than before. Finally, she realized that she was wanting to use God, to have Him do all the mothering things that Rob would not accept from her. And that was the problem. Rob was ready for more independence. He did not need or want as much mothering as Marianne thought she needed to give. When she finally realized that at least half of the conflict was over her own need to mother, rather than Rob's need for independence, she could just ask God to provide the best influences for Rob's spiritual, mental, emotional, and physical health and growth, consistent with what Rob was ready to accept. Then Marianne felt at peace.

It is possible that Rob subconsciously sensed that his mother was trying to control him through prayer, and that she subconsciously sensed his rejection of that control. This could have been the reason that her prayer left her more upset than before. When she moved to the point of "letting go and letting God" do the work in Rob's life, she exhibited a level of trust and faith in His love and wisdom that was very powerful.

Dr. Herb Puryear once gave the illustration that if a car were stalled on a road at night, no one would object to your stopping nearby and setting up flares to prevent oncoming traffic from colliding with it. However, if you decided to use your own car to push or pull the stalled vehicle from the road, you might well damage the brakes, transmission, or bumpers of the car in your attempt to help. The intended helpful influence would have turned to a destructive force because of the car's internal parts resisting your "help". In the same way, praying for someone contrary to that person's own will may make matters worse instead of better.

Our intercessory prayer can be strengthened if we pray with the correct attitude. When we are angry, jealous, resentful, or are experiencing evil or inappropriate sexual desires, we cannot express pure love, and the desired good effect of our prayer may not be felt. All these emotions partake of selfishness, and effective intercessory prayer is loving, and therefore selfless. Paul even said that he could pray for himself to be outcast from Christ for the sake of the Jews, if that would bring them to salvation (Romans 9:3). What an example of selfless love!

Even the most pure and powerful pray-er will admit that not all intercessory prayers are answered in the way (s)he would prefer. James says:

> Is anyone among you in trouble? He should turn to prayer.... Is one of you ill? He should send for the elders of the congregation to pray over him and anoint him with oil in the name of the Lord. The prayer offered in faith will save the sick man, the Lord will raise him from his bed, and any sins he may have committed will be forgiven. Therefore confess your sins to one another, and pray for one another, and then you will be healed. A good man's prayer is powerful and effective.
> (James 5:13-16, NEB)

The process sounds simple— except, perhaps, for the matter of finding elders of a church today who would take time from their schedules to go to a member's house and pray for him, not to mention being sufficiently scripturally oriented to anoint him with oil! And yet even following these instructions to the letter does not guarantee healing. For the most important factor in healing is the person being healed.

> Larry had always been a dedicated Christian. When he retired, he naturally started giving more time to his church work. For the first two years of his retirement, he almost made church-building maintenance work a full-time job.

Then his sister-in-law died, and he found out just how exhausting it could be to serve as executor for an estate. Next, his brother became ill, and Larry had to assume almost full responsibility for taking care of him. Occasionally he remarked to his family that he had given up on all his retirement plans, because other people were taking all his time. When he developed cancer, countless friends, family members, and church brothers and sisters prayed for him. But within six months, Larry died.

Why didn't all these combined prayers of faith save Larry's life? Perhaps because he himself had decided that he needed to die. He very likely did not realize this decision consciously, and would have denied it if he had been asked. But his closest friends knew that was what had happened. Regardless of the number of intercessors, God will not coerce someone into healing any problem. And neither can/should we. Not all prayer-resistant cases are as clear-cut as Larry's. Some people may resist healing because of a subconscious need for attention, or a hidden guilt feeling resulting in a need to suffer, or any of numerous other reasons. Indeed, when we are seeking our own healing through prayer or any other means, self-searching is usually in order to see if we have any blocks in the way of getting results. We must emphatically avoid any tendency to imply anything which may lead the sufferer to feelings of guilt. This is true even if we are all but certain that a person's attitudes are blocking healing, because guilt can only make the situation worse. We can never force another to change or grow; it's hard enough to force ourselves to do so. But if we recognize that these blocks to prayer exist, we can more easily understand the times when our prayers do not bring the results we expected. And we can pray for growth in any areas that may be blocking healing, always leaving the details to God.

But on no account are we to weaken our faith or stop praying just because the desired results were not achieved.

> He spoke to them in a parable to show that they should keep on praying and never lose heart: "There was once a judge who cared nothing for God or man, and in the same town there was a

widow who constantly came before him demanding justice against her opponent. For a long time he refused; but in the end he said to himself, 'True, I care nothing for God or man; but this widow is so great a nuisance that I will see her righted before she wears me out with her persistence.' " The Lord said, "You hear what the unjust judge says; and will not God vindicate his chosen, who cry out to him day and night, while he listens patiently to them? I tell you, he will vindicate them soon enough. But when the Son of Man comes, will he find faith on the earth?"
(Matthew 18:1-8, NEB)

This is a difficult parable, because at first glance we think God is being compared to an unjust judge. On closer examination, we find that Jesus is saying that if even an unjust human will do what is right because of a petitioner's persistence, then certainly God will. But notice the time: "He will vindicate them soon enough." Soon enough, that is, for God's purposes, not necessarily for our own. We are not to focus on the time, but on continuing to live in faith. We are to have faith— not in the desired result of our prayers— but in the person to Whom we pray! Developing and maintaining that faith is the subject of a later chapter.

The passage from James 5 that was quoted earlier has some additional vitally important advice that is too often ignored. Did you notice that it is after we confess our sins to one another and pray for one another that we are to expect healing? I confess to you that I do not often confess my sins to anyone! Do you? Why is this so important? Most obviously, because "confession is good for the soul." Spiritual teachers and modern psychologists alike know that when we express emotional concerns, we become better able to deal with them. (*Please* do not read this sentence as endorsing the have-a-tantrum school of behavioral therapy. After having tantrums whenever I darn well pleased throughout most of my early life, I finally learned that doing so made me feel worse, because I always made the people I loved unhappy. The ensuing shame and regret were far worse than any supposed relief I may have gained from the outburst. There are Biblical ways of dealing with anger.) Note that *express* means "push out". We push the roots of the strong emotions out into the light of discourse, and hopefully, empathy. We find that as we talk the things out, they're not so damning as they seemed. When we do this with a truly Christian friend, we also find that another human can mediate God's understanding and forgiveness.

Modern medical research has uncovered another aspect to James's advice. Researchers have concluded that people who feel "connected" to others have improved immune function and greater ability to heal themselves! To whom can you confess your sins? Only to someone you trust, someone to whom you feel connected. In the regular sharing of our failures with other Christians, we build up an environment that promotes health. James knew that 2000 years ago, and it's been staring us in the face ever since!

Now before you point out to me that I have strayed from the topic of intercession into the quest for personal healing, notice the second half of James's sentence: we are to confess our sins, and to pray for one another, **and then you will be healed**. Our own healing is directly tied to our practice of intercession. More than that, the implication is that of a group engaged in mutual support of a regular nature, as indicated by the tense of the Greek verbs, which really mean "keep on confessing" and "keep on praying." If our Sunday School classes worked in this way, being open and loving and concerned and trusting enough to confess sins to each other and to pray regularly for each other, I very strongly suspect that the members of the class would witness an outbreak of healing like the ones James apparently knew, that enabled him to say categorically, "and then you will be healed."

In addition to affirming the value of intercessory prayer, the Bible is very clear about the strength of united prayer. Again, if we limit our understanding of prayer's action to one of persuading God to do something, we build a picture of God that is untenable. He becomes a God who not only has to be roused to help people, but one who only bends to political pressure when there are numbers of people involved. Certainly this is not the correct understanding. Jesus has given us the clue in saying:

> Again I tell you this: if two of you agree on earth about any request you have to make, that request will be granted by my heavenly Father. For where two or three have met together in my name, I am there among them.
> (Matthew 18:19-20, NEB)

If Jesus is among us when we pray, and if we are attentive to his leading, then we are more likely to pray according to God's will. Naturally, this increases the power of our prayers.

Ritual Prayer

Christian beliefs about the value and place of ritual prayer run the gamut from the feeling that all prayer must be personal and informal to the conviction that all prayer must be conducted as a ritual. While we have no record of Jesus saying anything specific about ritual prayer, it is risky to argue from silence that He did not value ritual prayer. We know that Jewish worship involved a number of ritual prayers, especially in the feast day ceremonies such as Passover and the Feast of Booths (Tabernacles). So although our Lord did not specifically commend ritual prayer, neither did he argue against it in a society in which its use was commonplace.

Probably the best approach to evaluating ritual prayer is to identify first the purpose of ritual itself. When properly used, ritual is intended to increase a person's or a group's attunement with God. Just going into church helps most of us begin to focus more fully on God and less on our secular concerns. For some of us, wearing certain clothes, hearing a certain kind of music, and following a specific form of worship helps also. For others, these things can engender a sort of sleepy boredom that is more likely to cause slumber than attunement! That is why there are Orthodox worship services, very heavily steeped in ritual, redolent of incense, and almost hypnotic in their effect; and also there are Pentecostal meetings that emphasize spontaneity and individual response.

Different worship styles work for different Christians. The same is true for ritual prayer.

Let us go back to the relationship with earthly parents. We engage in certain rituals with them. There are birthday cards, for one thing. What good does it really do any of us to spend a few dollars to buy a card that tells a parent what he or she already knows? Yet it does do some good. That ritual speaks to the heart, to the emotions. Intellectually our parents *know* we love them, but the overpriced piece of stiff paper helps them to *feel* that we love them. If ritual prayer helps us to feel more in tune with God, then we should use it. If it brings on a feeling of stupor, then we should leave it alone.

There are two opposite mistakes we may make regarding ritual prayer, depending upon our personal tendencies. The first is for those who find the ritual useful to allow ritual prayer to replace "praying with the mind," as Paul describes it. If our total communication with our parents were mediated by Hallmark, we would be in a very sick relationship! The other mistake is for those who find no help in ritual to denigrate its use by those it aids. God honors our attempts to relate to Him in whatever way feels right to us.

Prayer for the Dead

Another form of prayer that has caused much infighting among Christians is prayer for the dead. Roman Catholic and Orthodox Christians believe in a purgatorial state that intervenes between physical death and entering into heaven. In 1 Corinthians 29, Paul speaks of people being baptized on behalf of the dead. He neither condones nor condemns the practice.

Most Protestants believe that each person is responsible for his own actions, and that the judgment cannot be swayed by the prayers of another. Numerous Scripture passages indicate that since salvation is by grace through faith, those who die in Christ are not judged. And yet we all have a sense that even though God accepts us completely through His grace (perhaps *because* He accepts us!) we somehow do not feel satisfied with the state of imperfection in which we all die. We feel instinctively that more work is needed before we are "conformed to the image of Christ". Some Christian denominations have adopted the idea of purgatory as a condition in which "everyone will be salted with fire." (Mark 9:49, NEB) But others rightly point out that this formulation goes beyond Scripture. The truth is, Scripture does not clearly tell us just what follows death, except that "we shall be like Him [Jesus], because we shall see Him as He is." (1 John 3:2b, NEB) I think that it is at least reasonable to assume that *some* experience awaits us after physical death, in which we will continue to grow. After all, the Kingdom is like a mustard seed, not a spoonful of instant coffee! If further learning does await us after physical death, then praying for those who have passed beyond physical life makes just as much sense as praying for those of us who haven't.

> Edward came from a close-knit family. When his uncle Arthur died, he felt the grief for awhile, but got over it. A year later, when his uncle Ben (his favorite uncle) died also, he had a rougher time. After five years, Edward's father died. Edward later mentioned to several friends that that summer passed almost without his noticing. As he began recovering from this latest emotional blow, the dreams began. Sometimes just his father was in the dream. Sometimes one or both of the uncles was with him. Once there was a very realistic dream in which former President Eisenhower spoke to Edward for awhile. Edward knew very well that his father had served under Ike during the Second World War, and that he admired him greatly. So even though this dream did not explicitly include any of his deceased family members, he considered it in the same category. The dreams bothered him. Nothing in them was frightening, but he could not help wondering whether they constituted premonitions of his own death. Then one day when he was meditating about these dreams, Edward was impressed to pray for his father and his uncles. He had never prayed for the dead, but he went ahead because the feeling was so strong. After praying for the comfort and well-being of his family members and asking God to assure them that he still loved them, Edward had a profound sense of peace. The dreams did not return.

Many people report having dreams about deceased loved ones. Often they find these dreams disturbing, as Edward did. If the simple act of praying for the dead can bring assurance and comfort to the deceased, then it is a wonderful thing to do. And if it only brings comfort to the person praying, that in itself is worthwhile. And certainly our Daddy will not be displeased if we do the best that our limited understanding permits.

Praying Without Ceasing

> Be joyful always. Pray without ceasing.
> (1 Thessalonians 5:17, Lamsa)

If we were completely honest about it, many of us would list the above passage as one of the most obscure or disturbing in the New Testament, depending upon how literally we took it. But there it is, anyway. If Paul had only meant "pray often," he would have said so. Yet how on earth can we pray without ceasing?

Once again we come back to the real meaning of prayer. It is attunement with our Heavenly Father. Praying without ceasing, then, is remaining attuned throughout our lives. While still requiring a major change in lifestyle for many of us, at least this understanding takes away the image of walking around with our eyes closed, mumbling to God! And it eliminates the daunting concept of trying to think of something to say to Him for all of our waking life. One of my favorite sayings is, "Peace is seeing a sunset and knowing Whom to thank." The very need to thank Him for "random acts of beauty" is a form of prayer. When we find ourselves troubled, and we immediately communicate in thought or word with God, we are praying. When we empathize with another person in his pain or trouble, and silently— perhaps even wordlessly— want Someone to help, we are praying.

So why make a fuss about praying without ceasing, if so much of our normal lives are really spent in prayer? Just this: while we may pray often, how many of us can say we do it unceasingly? When another driver cuts in front of us in traffic, is our response prayerful? When an attractive member of the opposite gender walks by on a beach, are our thoughts in attunement with God? When the outgo seems to be dwarfing the income, are our reactions those of prayer? Most of us can maintain a prayerful attitude when we are in church or taking in a glorious scene of nature. But Jesus could remain attuned to God under every circumstance of His life. And "We... possess the mind of Christ" (1 Cor. 2:16, NEB).

How then can we develop the ability to be always prayerful?

> Be still, and know that I am God. (Psalm 46:10, KJV)
> Wait quietly for the LORD, be patient till He comes; (Psalm 37:7, NEB)
> ...as for them who wait for Yahweh, they shall inherit the earth.
> (Psalm 37:9, Rhm)

What does it mean to "wait upon the LORD?" As we will soon discuss, the third stage of Christian meditation is waiting on God. After we relax and focus our minds on some affirmation of God's greatness or our oneness with Him, we then wait for Him to commune with us. Jesus's image in Revelation is of a table for two where we meet with our Master in the closest communion:

> Here I stand knocking at the door; if anyone hears my voice and opens the door, I will come in and sit down to supper with him and he with me.
> (Revelation 3:20, NEB)

To open the door, we must first clear out the rubbish of worldly concerns that are blocking the entry. The door is the portal of our minds, and that portal must be freed from the thousand clamors of our everyday concerns if we are to hear the still, small voice. Certainly this is not easy to do, and it is especially difficult when the demands on us are greatest. But upon first awakening in the morning, and before we eat our meals, and just before we go to sleep at night, if we are still and invite a "knowing" of God to fill us, we will slowly but steadily grow into the ability to be always prayerful.

The other key to a prayerful attitude is consistency. Have you ever dieted, or at least known someone who has? How often do we decide to lose some weight or to eat more healthfully, only to abandon ourselves to a periodic binge? How often do we decide to undertake a particular spiritual discipline, such as daily prayer or Bible reading, only to abandon it when we feel especially busy? How often do we decide to give up a weakness or vice, only to give in to it again and again? As we practice consistency, we grow spiritually. When we give in to our lower desires, we slip backward. In some political campaigns, much is made of the issue of integrity. A person with integrity is "the same yesterday, today, and forever"; "with him there is no variation, no shadow of turning"— sound like Anybody you know?

Developing consistency requires patience— not stolid endurance, but the patience that understands the purposes and growth opportunities of every event of life, and uses the resources of the present to manage them. When we are faced with a challenge, we can respond in many ways. We can be angry at the intrusion upon our lives. We can be resigned to the inevitability of trouble. We can look for scapegoats to blame for the event. We can try to ignore it and hope it will go away. Or we can look upon it as... well, a challenge, an opportunity for growth, a chance to improve our abilities in yet another arena. This last way is the way of patience. It is the way that leads us to stick with our goals until we have achieved them. It is the way that leads to consistency, through which we learn more and more to attune to God unceasingly. "By your patience you will gain your souls." (Luke 21:19, Lamsa)

Christian Meditation

I think I first heard the word *meditation* when I was about seven. Asking for a definition, I was told it meant "thinking about something". My high-school and college years occurred during the 1960's. During that time, largely because of the influence of George Harrison and others of the Beatles, Eastern (mainly Indian) religious thought was introduced to a generation of Americans. *Meditation* came to mean one of the forms of meditation that are practiced in Buddhism. Gradually, some of us Christians learned that there is a rich heritage of meditation in the Christian church, going all the way back to the beginning. We have already mentioned that much of Jesus's time in prayer was probably "tuning in" to our Father; this really constitutes meditation. Notice how many times in Psalms such as Psalm 119 meditation is mentioned. From books like those mentioned on page 108, we can learn something about this too-long-neglected form of prayer.

The essence of meditation can be summarized in the statement: "Prayer is talking to God; meditation is listening to Him." We have defined prayer as attuning ourselves to God, so according to our definition, meditation becomes a special class of prayer. We listen to God in the same way that we listen to any other friend, by quieting ourselves physically, focusing on God, and becoming mentally expectant.

Just as we would not expect to hear a human friend talk with us when we are mowing a lawn, we can best hear God if we find a place that is quiet and free from distractions. Some people can meditate in their offices or dining rooms, but many others find that everyday items in these rooms call too much attention to "things to do". Thus it is often helpful to select a special place whose ambiance does not suggest everyday demands. It also helps to set aside a particular time each day to meditate. Habit can be a powerful ally!

We begin to meditate by quieting our physical selves. The specific position is not important, so long as it is one in which we can relax and be comfortable. Because our bodies are not used to being quiet, and will alert us to minor stiffness or discomfort, we can help the physical stage of meditation by doing some gentle body movements— *exercises* is too strenuous a word. Mild stretches and head-and-neck rolls are usually very good.

Some people find that specific music or smells help them to meditate, or having just bathed, or loosening any tight clothing. (A whole subset of the music industry has grown up around so-called "meditation music". Bach, Handel, Mozart, and the other great masters are at least as good, and often better.) The general idea is to pay attention to your body and do whatever you feel will make you more comfortable and relaxed. If you have studied some special relaxation exercise such as Autogenic training or progressive relaxation, and find this helps you to relax, that's fine, too.

The only special precaution here is not to try to meditate when you're tired or upset. When you're tired, you'll likely fall asleep as soon as you fully relax. While this may be what you need, it is not meditation! When you're upset, the attempt at meditation is often lost in worrying.

The second stage of Christian meditation is very different from the second stage of other forms of meditation. Transcendental Meditation uses a mantra such as the syllable *Om* or a complex symbolic drawing to distract the conscious mind and promote a change in the state of consciousness. Christian meditation seeks to focus the conscious mind on God. The difference is the same as the difference between just sailing a boat, and sailing the boat to a planned destination. Christians recognize the fact that there are other spiritual influences than God, and we do not want to grant these influences access to our subconscious minds. (Some Christians call these negative influences "evil spirits," and others call them "the shadow self" or another psychological name, but we recognize their existence.) Therefore, after we become physically quiet, we first pray a prayer of protection, asking Jesus that any ideas or images that come into our minds during the meditation be from God only. Next, we focus our minds on something that represents God for us. I personally think that Jesus gave His disciples the Lord's Prayer for this specific purpose. Some people like to focus only on a single phrase of the Prayer, such as "Our Father," letting their minds range over all the things implied by this address. The next day, they might focus on "Hallowed be Thy Name." Others use a favorite Bible verse that seems to them to capture the essence of God. Remember, this stage is focusing, not analyzing. Perhaps *feeling* is a better word. When we say, "I am thinking about Tom," we often are concentrating on the feeling we experience in Tom's presence, not analyzing his actions or personality. The idea in this stage is to use the principle of replacement: we cannot "not think" about something. If we try, a thousand other some things will enter our minds to distract us. But we can choose to think about a particular thing. Since we want to attune to God, we think about Him.

At first, the mind will rebel from our efforts to concentrate. We will find all sorts of aches and pains, obligations both important and trivial, and even snatches of songs and poems that will come to mind. It is a mistake to fight these images. Instead, we just recognize them and set them aside, or, as one teacher suggests, "Just smile at them and return to your focus." This is a process we use often anyway. "Yes, I know, but I'll deal with that later," is a familiar thought to each of us. Calmness and patience with ourselves is the key.

After we have spent some time focusing on God, it will feel right for us to move to an attitude of expectancy. When the telephone rings, and we hear the voice of a familiar friend, we feel a pleasant expectancy as we wait for him or her to speak to us. It is natural to feel the same as we wait on God. Sometimes, we will be dealing with a particular question or problem in our lives on which we want God's help. At other times, we simply want fellowship with Him. In either case, we wait. At this point, Jesus's promise, "I am with you always," (from Matthew 28:20) is a great blessing. Very few people ever physically hear God speak to them. Most of us must simply "Be still and know that I am God" (Psalm 46:10, KJV). If we are accustomed to the awareness of the Lord's presence always, it is much easier to feel His presence in meditation. But even when we think we are spiritually drained and cannot really feel Him near, He is. The Bible is full of promises of His presence. Many of these promises have already been quoted in this book. They must become real for us, and they do that only as we live them. If my accountant says that I should fill in a tax form a certain way, and file it at a certain time, I do so whether I feel like it or not. If my God says He is near me, I believe it whether I feel like it or not! To meditate as a Christian, I must live as a Christian. My God is One. I must be one also, not many scattered personalities, some of which claim to believe in God, and others of which give primary weight to my feelings. I believe that if I open the door, He will come in and we will sit down at the table for two. Since I want that fellowship with Him, I will practice opening the door. This is meditation.

Many people report great spiritual experiences resulting from meditation. John was meditating when he received the Revelation. "I was in the spirit on the Lord's day... " (Revelation 1:10a). Of course some of these people, like John, are called "saints," but many more are just ordinary folks. These special experiences are gifts from God in response to particular needs in these people's lives and ministries. They do not come on command, nor are they brought on by intense desire. Some meditators become discouraged and give up because they never seem to have a "peak" experience. It makes no more sense than for a person who is healthy to mourn because she has not experienced a miraculous cure from cancer. God will give us what we need. If it is just the knowledge that we are setting aside time to be with Him, it is enough.

Just as there comes a time when we move from focusing to expectancy, there also comes a time when it feels right for the meditation session to end. We may just gradually begin again to notice the world around us, we may want to say a mental "amen", or in some other appropriate way bring the session to a close. But one thing still remains. In the process of meditation, we invite the Lord to enter our minds and visit. When Jesus walked the earth, His presence caused even His robe to have such power that it inspired faith to heal the woman with hemorrhages (Luke 8:43 ff). People would seek merely to stand within the shadows of Peter and the other apostles so that they would be healed (Acts 5:15,16). Handkerchiefs were brought to Paul for him to touch so that others could touch them and be healed (Acts 19:12). All this was the natural result of the power of God. Peter and Paul were not any more special than you and I.

> Peter... [told the people] "Why stare at us as though we had made this man walk by some power or godliness of our own?... The name of Jesus, by awakening faith, has strengthened this man, whom you see and know, and this faith has made him completely well, as you can all see for yourselves."
> (excerpted from Acts 3:12b-16, NEB)

If we have opened ourselves to the power of God, we need to use that power or energy that has been raised in meditation. We do that by intercessory prayer. I strongly suspect that the reason James tied intercession with receiving healing (in the passage from James 5 quoted earlier) was this very need. After we have been with the Lord, we are best equipped to do the Lord's work!

Praying in Jesus's Name

Indeed anything you ask in my name I will do it,
so that the Father may be glorified in the Son.
(John 14:13, NEB)

Again and again we find Jesus telling us to ask in His name. If most of us would admit it, we find this advice enigmatic, at best. What does it mean to pray "in His name"? For the answer, we must look back at first-century society, and then we will find some familiar parallels in our own society.

Up until modern times throughout the world— and even in modern times in some societies— the family was the building block of society. (Some would say that we have erred in making the individual the building block of Western society, but that's another topic!) Carrying on the family name was extremely important. As discussed on page 43, an adult son could act in his father's name. Even if a son were to go to another city where he was not known, but the father was known and the son could prove the relationship, he could still act in his father's name. Notice that it's the relationship that is crucial. If we expect it to mean anything that we ask something in Jesus's name, we must have a vital relationship with Him. This goes right back to visiting with Him in prayer and meditation.

When I was in the sixth grade, I had a very close friend whose past was not exactly comforting to my parents. He came from a shattered family with an alcoholic father, and had spent time in training schools. While he never was the bad influence that my folks feared he would be, he did have certain habits of speech that were not in keeping with my Baptist upbringing. I picked up some of these habits. It is human nature to pick up traits from those with whom we spend time. When we spend time with Jesus, we become more like Him. Then what we ask for in prayer is much more likely to be within His will. In this sense, asking in His name is not using a specific ritual phrase as we conclude a prayer; it is asking as He Himself would ask.

Try as we might, we cannot make Jesus's promise to answer our prayers into a magic formula to cajole Him into seeing things our way. It is instead a formula for living so that our will is aligned with His, and thus our prayers are what He would pray in the same situation.

Careful readers will have noticed that in this section we have gone back and forth between the ideas of praying to the Father and praying to Jesus. To whom do Christians pray? On the one hand, Jesus Himself always prayed to His Daddy. On the other hand, He told us that He is knocking at the door of our consciousness, and that He desires to be invited in. He told the disciples:

> When a man believes in me, he believes in him who sent me rather than in me; seeing me, he sees him who sent me.
> (John 12:44-45, NEB)

> Anyone who has seen me has seen the Father.
> (John 14:9b, NEB)

Did Jesus mean that He Himself embodies the entirety of God? No, because He also said:

> ... [I]t is for your good that I am leaving you. If I do not go, your Advocate will not come, whereas if I go, I will send him to you. When he comes, he will confute the world, and show where right and wrong and judgment lie. He will convict them of wrong, by their refusal to believe in me; he will convince them that right is on my side, by showing that I go to the Father when I pass from your sight; and he will convince them of divine judgment, by showing that the prince of this world stands condemned.
> (John 16:7-11, NEB)

In this brief passage, Jesus tells us of the supremacy of the Father, the sacrificial love of the Son, and the counseling of the Holy Spirit. No part of the Trinity by itself is a sufficient representation of the glory of God. The limited nature of our perception requires all three for us to even approach an adequate understanding. I pray to the Father for guidance, fellowship, and the assurance that the world— and my life— are under control. When I feel a particular need to sense understanding of some worldly problem, or when I just need a Brother, I pray to Jesus. As I write this very page, or when I talk to a friend or student who is in need, or as I teach a Sunday school class, I count on the working of the Holy Spirit within me. But as I do each of these, I know that all three— Father, Son, and Holy Spirit— are One. And the great holy mystery is that I am invited to become one with Him!

Faith

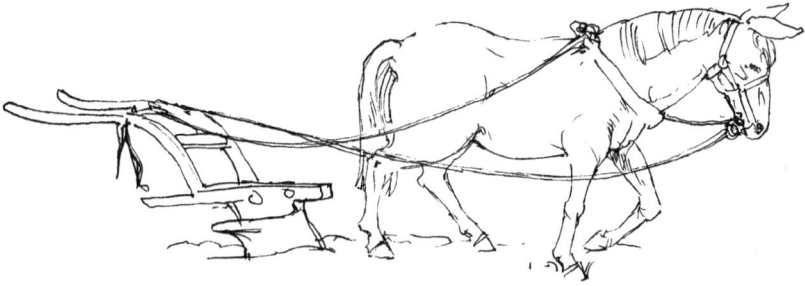

Some people define faith as "believing what you know isn't true". While this definition may make us smile, its accuracy as a working definition for many Christians is no laughing matter. The Greek will have none of this. *Pistis* is the word usually translated "faith", and it means confidence, certainty, trust, and guarantee or assurance, as in the sense of an oath. How can God expect us to believe implicitly in something that we haven't seen? Can we psyche ourselves into that kind of belief? Would it be intellectually honest for us to do so? These questions outline some of the problems that thinking Christians have always had with the concept of faith. And yet we know that "without faith it is impossible to please him [God]" (Hebrews 11:6, NEB). There must be a key to this paradox.

First, we must recognize that we *all, always* live by faith. We eat certain foods and not others because we have faith in people who have told us what is and is not safe to eat. I have never seen nor heard of anyone knowingly eating poison ivy, to find out whether it is really unsafe. We pay hard-earned money to lawyers so that they will write long documents in (to us) semi-comprehensible language, because we have faith that they know how to ensure that after we die, our possessions will go to our chosen beneficiaries. For centuries, people would even take doses of harmful chemicals or allow leeches to suck their blood because of faith in the medical superstitions of the time. When we believe something enough to act upon it, we are exercising faith.

Faith and wishing are not the same. We can wish that we were physically fit, but unless we go and act upon that wish by eating properly and exercising regularly, the wish has no substance. We can psyche ourselves into believing that our wishes have come true, but if that goes against objective facts (what most folks actually observe to be true), then we have only succeeded in self-delusion.

So where does faith come from? The first person who ever told me that poison ivy was not good to eat was my mother. I had faith that what she said was true, for two reasons. First, all the evidence that I had ever seen led me to conclude that she was trustworthy and wanted the best for me: *I knew her.* Second, my experience with disregarding her advice was usually painful. So my faith in my mother was based upon relationship and experience. If a neighbor had contradicted my mother, I would have rejected his opinion out of hand, because of my superior relationship with her.

Now there are many things that we each have learned by experience, so we need not accept them on faith alone. Those things for which we depend upon faith are the ones for which personal verification would be dangerous, difficult, or impossible. Faith in God is the same. We have faith because we know God. But this kind of knowing is one that does not directly involve the physical senses, and therefore demands a greater sensitivity of the spiritual senses. God has placed in our hearts the instinct to believe in a Creator. The evidence is present in the orderliness of His creation. The Gospel, shared with us by people with whom we have relationships of trust, tells us that God wants communion with us. We see our own need for communion with our children, and we understand. We have faith in God, first, because we trust people who tell us of Him. Then we develop that faith by our own experience as we listen to His voice in our inner promptings. The faith is shaped by the concrete teachings of Jesus, and as we better see our Father in our minds' eyes, the faith grows. "We conclude that faith is awakened by the message, and the message that awakens it comes through the word of Christ" (Romans 10:17, NEB). As we study the word of Christ, our faith grows. Exercising faith is not some Herculean effort by which we will ourselves to "believe", but simply choosing to focus our minds on the present realities and future hopes to which our faith carries us.

Perhaps you have read of Glenn Cunningham, the athlete whose legs were badly burned in his youth. Pitting his faith in his ability to walk, then run again, against the doctors' predictions that he would never walk again, he not only walked but became an Olympic champion runner.

A later Olympic runner, Roger Bannister, broke the world record by running the mile in less than four minutes. Once he had broken this speed barrier that had stood as long as Olympic records were kept, several other runners in various places bettered his time. Their faith had not been quite up to the level of Bannister's, in that the four-minute barrier was real to them. Once he had shown that it could be broken, their faith-barrier came down, and they also ran the mile in less than four minutes.

In physics, two properties that are alike yet sort of opposite are called *duals*. Right and left are duals. Up and down are duals. In electricity, capacitance and inductance are duals. Faith has a dual; it is called fear.

> One summer evening Art was watching TV while his children played in the front yard. Suddenly his attention was captured by the screech of brakes. As he bounded to the door, his mind was already filling with pictures of a bleeding child having been struck by a car. But when he opened the door, he saw both children happily playing marbles. The car had driven on down the street, with no obvious reason for its abrupt stop. As Art returned to his TV show, his heart was still racing, his hands and feet were cold, his stomach was knotted, and the metallic taste of fear filled his mouth. Yet there was no objective reason for these symptoms.

Art had created a terrifying scenario from the force of his own fear, and was bearing the physical consequences of this very real manifestation of his fear. Had he had a weak heart, his fear might even have killed him.

> And what is faith? Faith gives substance to our hopes, and makes us certain of realities we do not see.
> (Hebrews 11:1, NEB)

In the preceding example, reality was brought into existence by faith or fear. Some people say, "Oh, faith is just subjective," not noticing that we live in subjectivity. If I feel strong, relaxed, and confident, my cardiovascular system and my immune system will perform at full capacity. If I feel weak and sick, I will act weak and sick. If I feel afraid, my physiological responses will reflect that fear. My belief, whether positive (faith) or negative (fear), will give substance to my expectations.

This brings us to hope. Like faith, *hope* does not mean "wishing". In the *Theological Dictionary of the New Testament*, Kittel and Friedrich state,

> When fixed on God, hope embraces expectation, trust, and patient waiting. It is linked to faith, as in Heb. 1:11, which stresses the certainty of what is divinely given.
> (one-volume abridged version, 1974, p.231)

If faith is the substance of the life we build, then hope is the blueprint. Faith without hope is substance without shape. Hope without faith is blueprint without bricks.

Hope also has a dual; it is worry. We could truly say that fear is the substance of things worried about! Dr. Norman Vincent Peale told the story of Gem Gilbert, a famous English tennis star of an earlier generation, who was petrified of going to the dentist. She often told her friends that if she were to have to go to a dentist's office it would kill her. At one point when she was in her 30's and otherwise in perfect health, her teeth had begun giving her so much trouble that her friends arranged for a dentist to come to her house. As soon as the examination was begun, Gem had a fatal heart attack. Her doctors agreed that there was no medical reason for the heart attack except fear. Thirty-plus years of worrying about a dentist's chair had built an image so powerful that it allowed the fear to actually kill her.

Thinking Christians often raise an objection whenever faith is discussed: if we can have whatever we ask for in faith, how can our decisions have any real meaning? In other words, why can't we use faith to avoid reaping what we sow? This was partially answered in section 3 of chapter 10: a greater cause can supercede the effect of a lesser cause. If we have learned our lesson from a mistake, that learning, coupled with God's grace, constitute a greater cause that can override the effect of our error.

To further answer this objection, we must first remember that we have faith *in God.*

> Ray's daughter Ann was three years old. One morning she was sitting in the bed in Ray's bedroom while Ray finished dressing. Suddenly, without warning, Ray heard, "Here I come, Daddy!" Turning around, he barely had time to catch the small bundle who had launched herself from the bed at him.

Ann had faith in Ray. She did not have some abstract thing called "faith" that meant she could have whatever she wanted. She believed in her daddy, that he would not allow her to be hurt. (Given Ann's age, she probably didn't imagine that there was anything he could not do to keep her safe!) If we have faith in our Daddy, rather than in some specific prayer answer that we have proposed, we leave the way open for Him to act in our best interest.

The Power of Faith

> Have faith in God. I tell you this: if anyone says to this mountain, "Be lifted from your place and hurled into the sea," and has no inward doubts, but believes that what he says is happening, it will be done for him. I tell you, then, whatever you ask for in prayer, believe that you have received it and it will be yours. (Mark 11:22-24, NEB)

This passage is read in all Christian churches, but believed in very few. The problem is that we cannot mentally picture anything as big as a mountain being thrown into the sea. "Has anyone ever done this?" we might ask. Surely such a feat would be recorded. Maybe Jesus was using hyperbole. Let's examine this question more closely.

First, the question of hyperbole. Can you think of any other instance in Scripture in which Jesus used hyperbole, or extreme exaggeration, for effect? Likening a rich man's entry into heaven to a camel passing through the eye of a needle would constitute hyperbole. However,

Dr. George M. Lamsa, who is a native speaker of Syriac (a modern-day descendant of Aramaic) as well as a renowned Bible scholar, says that we have mistranslated that passage. The Aramaic words for "rope" and "camel" differ by only one tiny vowel marking. Passing a rope through the eye of a needle provides an image that emphasizes the need for a puffed-up rich man to learn some humility, and probably is still hyperbole. Jesus uses this saying to emphasize the danger of trust in riches, which did not seem sinful to His hearers, especially since their society considered riches a clear sign of God's blessing. But the disciples already considered miracles as great things far beyond their capacity. Would the master teacher exaggerate a point that was already unbelievable to the disciples? I think not. I believe we can rule out hyperbole.

Now what if Jesus had said, "If anyone says to this pebble, 'roll over three times,' it will happen." Most of us would find this easier to believe. But what Jesus is saying is that the spiritual reality tapped by prayer is superior to the physical reality to which we are most accustomed. What if a first-century physicist had said, "If you could release the energy trapped in one gram of matter, you could plow 3 billion wheat fields." Aside from the fact that the gram was undefined then, no one would have even taken him seriously. Yet today, after we have seen the immense energy released by a nuclear explosion, we can accept this statement as fact. Our understanding of physical reality is superior to that of anyone in the first century. Jesus's understanding of spiritual reality is certainly superior to that of anyone before or since. In our own time, we have seen Uri Geller demonstrate the ability to bend spoons by mental energy[8], and Ingo Swann able to alter the field inside a remotely located, superconductively shielded magnetometer[9]. Qualitatively, moving mountains is no different. It's only a matter of scale. Is it possible

---

[8]Russel Targ and Harold Puthoff, *Mind Reach* (New York: Delacorte, 1977), 139-145.

[9]Ibid., 19-45.

that the scale, or the amount of matter involved, does not even matter?

Now to the question of whether anyone has ever thrown a mountain into the sea by command. I can imagine only one reason that anyone would do such a thing, and that is to find out whether (s)he could. But a person with sufficient faith to achieve the task would not need to find out; (s)he would know. I think it's somewhat like the gas mileage of a Rolls-Royce: if you have to ask, you don't need to know. But great feats of faith are in great evidence in the field of medicine, as in many other fields. Those who do not have eyes to see call them coincidences and ignore them. Many writings of great Christians witness the power of faith; you just have to look in order to find them.

> In truth, in very truth I tell you, he who has faith in me will do what I am doing; and he will do greater things still because I am going to the Father. Indeed anything you ask in my name I will do, so that the Father may be glorified in the Son. If you ask anything in my name I will do it. (John 14:12-14, NEB)

This is another teaching of Jesus that far too few Christians believe. "How," we may ask, "can we do greater things than Jesus did?" First, we need to remember that Jesus was fully human.

> His state was divine
> yet he did not cling
> to his equality with God
> but emptied himself
> to assume the condition of a slave, and became
> as men are;
> and being as all men are, he was humbler yet,
> even to accepting death,
> death on a cross.
> (Philippians 2:6-8, JB)

The only way that He could really be The Way for us is for Him to have been entirely human. If He had a secret link to God that is not available to us, then it is unfair for God to expect us to "... attain to the unity inherent in our faith and our knowledge of the Son of God—to mature manhood, measured by nothing less than the full stature of Christ" (Ephesians 4:13, NEB). Being fully human, Jesus performed His miracles through the same means as the Old Testament prophets. In fact, if you'll read about Elisha, you'll find that He also healed lepers, fed large groups from small provisions, and raised the dead. But after the resurrection, Jesus sent the Holy Spirit to dwell within us individually and corporately. This is the source of the greater power available to us.

Developing Faith

You have faith. I have faith. We live by faith all the time. Yet most Christians feel a need to develop their faith. There seems to be a paradox here, so let's look more closely. As I sit at my computer typing, I have a great deal of faith that if the phone rings, I can walk across the room to answer it. In fact, I do not know with certainty that I can do so. As soon as I stand up, I could turn my ankle, or we could have an earthquake, or a thousand other things could prevent my answering the phone. But I have faith, based upon my having gotten up and answered the phone many times before.

I have only used my lawyer to draw up legal papers for me. If I were unjustly accused of some crime, I *think* that he could successfully defend me, but I would have some trepidation about the matter, since I have had no experience with him (or anyone else, for that matter) in such a situation.

Most Christians, though tragically not all, believe firmly that God's best awaits them after physical death. We have experience using our faith in believing for our salvation. (If you are not absolutely convinced of your salvation, but think that it's always some sort of cosmic crapshoot until your actual death, stop right now and read Romans 10:9-10, Ephesians 2:8-10, and 2 Corinthians 5:21. Even though we can choose to accept and follow Christ, or we can choose to reject his salvation, we cannot, while honestly trying to follow him, slip up and lose our salvation. The Puritans were dead wrong on this!) But many of us have not experienced the use of faith in other areas. We believe Christ for our salvation, as I believe my lawyer for writing a will, but we only have a vague notion that somehow he may help with our emotional, physiological, financial, or social needs, just as I have only a vague notion about my lawyer's abilities in criminal court.

So how do we build up our faith? Just as we would build up a muscle: by feeding it and by using it.

Feeding Our Faith

We feed our faith by studying the Bible, especially the New Testament and the Prophets. We also feed it by making special effort to read or hear contemporary reports of the action of faith in people's lives. And we feed it by learning the laws under which faith works.

Biblical Evidence

Most Christians are familiar with the miracles that occurred in the lives of Abraham, Joseph, and Moses. Less well-known are the miracles of Elijah and Elisha.

> When he [Elijah] reached the entrance to the village, he saw a widow gathering sticks, and he called to her and said, "Please bring me a little water in a pitcher to drink." As she went to fetch it, he called after her, "Bring me, please, a piece of bread as well." But she said, "As the LORD your God lives, I have no food to sustain me except a handful of flour in a jar and a little oil in a flask. Here I am, gathering two or three sticks to go and cook something for my son and myself before we die." "Never fear," said Elijah; "go and do as you say, but first make me a small cake from what you have and bring it out to me; after that make something for your son and yourself. For this is the word of the LORD the God of Israel: 'The jar of flour shall not give out nor the

> flask of oil fail, until the LORD sends rain on the
> land.' "
>
> She went and did as Elijah had said, and there
> was food for him and for her and her family for a
> long time. The jar of flour did not give out nor
> did the flask of oil fail, as the word of the LORD
> had foretold through Elijah.
> (I Kings 17:10-16, NEB)

In showing faith by helping a traveler in need, at what she might have
thought great cost to herself and her son, the widow saw a miracle of
multiplication, reminding us of Jesus's feeding the four thousand and
the five thousand. In subsequent verses we read of Elijah calling the
widow's son back to life, the prophet's powerful vindication of
Yahweh on Mount Carmel, and then his own despair when he lets his
vision fail, taking in the political situation from an earthly perspective.
We see the miracles of Elijah, but we also come to know the prophet,
warts and all.

The story of Elisha and the Shunamite woman is an endearing one.
Perhaps the most astounding part recounts the sudden death of her
son and Elisha's subsequent visit to her home.

> When Elisha entered the house, there was the
> boy dead, on the bed where he had been laid. He
> went into the room, shut the door on the two of
> them and prayed to the LORD. Then, getting on
> to the bed, he lay upon the child, put his mouth
> to the child's mouth, his eyes to his eyes and his
> hands to his hands; and, as he pressed upon him,
> the child's body grew warm. Elisha got up and
> walked once up and down the room; then,
> getting on to the bed again, he pressed upon him
> and breathed into him seven times; and the boy
> opened his eyes. The prophet summoned Gehazi
> and said, "Call this Shunamite woman." She
> answered his call and the prophet said, "Take

your child." She came in and fell prostrate before
him. Then she took up her son and went out.
(2 Kings 4:32-37, NEB)

If we read carefully the stories of the monarchy in Israel and Judah,
we learn that there was a group called "the sons of the prophets" of
whom Elijah and Elisha were leaders. However, the group was well-
established by the time of Saul (see 1 Samuel 10), and lasted long
after Elisha died. In fact the Essenes of Jesus's time considered
themselves to be a continuation of this same group. Apparently there
was some specific training in prayer and fasting, along with a
particular lifestyle that encouraged sensitivity to the will and power of
God.

Several of the miracles of Jesus have already been recounted in this
book. Probably you are familiar with others. There were miracles of
healing, miracles of multiplication, miracles of financial provision,
and miracles of restoration to life. Actually, Jesus performed
essentially the same sorts of miracles that the prophets before him
had performed.

Much has been written claiming that Jesus's miracles were only signs
to inspire faith. This theology comes from a limited reading of John.
Throughout his Gospel, he refers to the miracles as signs. However, a
careful reading of the entire New Testament record reveals that Jesus
performed many, if not most miracles from a sense of compassion.
Six times in the Gospel of Matthew alone we are told that Jesus was
moved by compassion. This point is critical. If Jesus performed
miracles only as signs, then we cannot count on their availability
when we need them. But if He performed them because He was
moved by compassion, we can believe for miracles in our own lives
also. Why would Jesus instruct us to have faith that anything is
possible for God if the miraculous was limited to his earthly ministry
alone?
In fact, Jesus said,

This is a wicked generation. It demands a sign,
and the only sign that will be given it is the sign
of Jonah.

(Luke 11:29, NEB)

Sadly, the "miracles were only signs" theology has dealt a death blow to the faith of countless Christians.

In the book of Acts, we find the stories of Peter's healing the cripple at the Beautiful Gate of the Temple (Acts 3:1-10), his miraculous release from prison (Acts 12:1-17), and numerous other extraordinary events. The church became so well-known as miracle-workers that:

> ... the sick were actually carried out into the streets and laid there on beds so the shadow of Peter might fall on one or another as he passed by; and the people from the towns round Jerusalem flocked in, bringing those who were ill or harassed by unclean spirits, and all of them were cured.
> (Acts 5:15-16, NEB)

Paul, too, manifested the power of God through his faith, by healing and other acts. I particularly love the story in Acts 20 in which Paul was preaching to a roomful of folk where many oil lamps were lighted. Probably because of the lack of oxygen, a young man named Eutychus fell asleep and dropped from a third-story window to the ground and was picked up for dead. Paul stopped the sermon, went downstairs, threw himself upon the boy, seizing him in his arms, and restored him to life. Then he went on preaching as if nothing had happened!

A careful reading of the writings of the earliest Church fathers and their opponents alike reveals an astonishing fact: miraculous healing was an acknowledged fact among the Christians up until the end of the second century. The decline of accounts of the miraculous after that time led Martin Luther to consider divine healing to be a "special dispensation" or favor from God, sent to get the church started. There is a better explanation, but one which Luther could not accept. It was that as the church became less radical and more socially acceptable, reported healings began to decrease. By the time of Constantine, during whose reign Christianity became the state religion, healings had nearly stopped altogether. Then for over a millennium the church was identified with secular power and increasing corruption. Those radicals who arose from time to time to call for a return to purer ways were denounced as heretics. Paul said, "The kingdom of God is not a matter of talk, but of power" (I Corinthians 4:20, NEB). For two hundred years the church proclaimed and lived in that power, but then it yielded to the seduction of Mammon.

When I was in college, we were required to take two religion courses. Most students took Old Testament and New Testament. I took Old Testament and World Religions. The reason for not taking New Testament was that I looked through the textbook and decided that I wanted none of what its author was saying. Specifically, in every section in which the Bible tells of a miracle, the author of the textbook went to great lengths to explain it away. According to him, those who came to Jesus to be healed or to be delivered from demons were victims of what psychologists used to call "hysterical" illnesses. Jesus was very good at spotting this type of case and through his great personality was able to set them at peace, healing their ailments. As a collegian, I thought this was hogwash; now I see it as ineffective hogwash. For even allowing the possibility that all the healings were psychosomatic, any modern psychologist would readily agree that healing such a case with a single office visit would in itself be a miracle!

Many of our present-day pastors and teachers in the church took such courses as the one I opted to avoid. We must therefore be on the lookout for such unbelief even in the teaching of very dedicated Christians, because they received faulty doctrine at a very impressionable time in their lives. In an attempt to make our theology respectable in the eyes of the world, an unfortunately large number of authors and teachers have substituted "for the doctrines of God the commandments of men" (Matthew 15:9, Isaiah 29:13). Paul warns us of the impossibility of ever making Christianity look respectable by worldly standards.

> This doctrine of the cross is sheer folly to those
> on their way to ruin, but to us who are on the

> way to salvation it is the power of God. Scripture says, "I will destroy the wisdom of the wise, and bring to nothing the cleverness of the clever." Where is your wise man now, your man of learning, or your subtle debater— limited, all of them, to this passing age? God has made the wisdom of this world look foolish. As God in his wisdom ordained, the world failed to find him by its wisdom, and he chose to save those who have faith by the folly of the Gospel.
> (1 Corinthians 1:18-21, NEB)

> Make no mistake about this: if there is anyone among you who fancies himself wise— wise, I mean, by the standards of this passing age— he must become a fool to gain true wisdom. For the wisdom of this world is folly in God's sight.
> (1 Corinthians 3:18-20, NEB)

The danger is that we will make intellectual respectability a god, sacrificing our faith in the Gospel on its altar. In fact, this is precisely what the textbook authors did. They made the common mistake of assuming that the world view of the present age is correct, and that of the first-century Christians was unschooled, illiterate, and superstitious. What immense blind egotism! We must remember that we always look at things through the blinders of our age, or through a glass, darkly. So, of course, did the writers of the New Testament, but they knew it, and they wrote under inspiration from the One who could see plainly. The veracity of their work has been proven in every age since.

We must not leave this survey of Biblical evidence of the power of faith without mentioning the great faith chapter, Hebrews 11. Back in chapter 6, the writer of Hebrews announced that (s)he was about to "stop discussing the rudiments of Christianity," and "advance toward maturity". A crucial part of this advance is a discussion of the many things that can be accomplished by faith. As you read chapter 11, notice that:

- Faith gives substance to our hopes.
- By faith we comprehend creation: the visible coming from the invisible Word.
- By faith Enoch passed from this life to the next without dying.
- By faith Noah and Abraham heard God's direction and acted upon it.
- By faith Sarah conceived when most people her age were dead.
- By faith Abraham offered Isaac in the knowledge that God would bring him back. (Notice that in Genesis 22:5-8, Abraham tells his servants, "Stay here with the ass while the boy and I go over there [to the place of sacrifice]; and when we have worshipped we will come back to you." Notice that Abraham did not say "*I* will come back to you." Also, when Isaac asked about the beast for the sacrifice, Abraham responded, "God will provide himself with a young beast for a sacrifice, my son." [NEB] Abraham *knew* the power of God and trusted fully in it.)

The list goes on. It has been called a roll-call of the faithful. But it is much more: it is a partial catalog of the blessings that can accrue from the exercise of faith. It could be called a sample-book of miracles.

Experiential and Contemporary Evidence

So I believe in miracles. What personal experience do I have to support my belief, so that it has become experiential, not merely hearsay or superstition?

1. About two years after my wife and I were married, we had our first really serious money crisis. This was the "where's-the-rent-money-coming-from" kind of crisis. We sat down and figured out exactly how much more we needed in the next six months than I was making. At that time, neither of

us had been active as Christians in some time, and in fact we were not sure just how much we believed of what we'd been taught in church as children. However, we did believe in a loving God, so we decided to pray together. This was our first prayer together ever. As we were saying "Amen", the phone rang. At the other end was an acquaintance from the office who had been teaching an evening class at a nearby technical college. He would not be able to teach the class the following term, so the dean had asked him to recommend a replacement. Teaching this particular class required a First Class Commercial FCC license, and I was one of the few people my friend knew who had one, so he called me. The stipend for teaching the class was precisely the amount we had just decided we needed. And by the way, the friend's last name was Shepherd! Is it easier to believe in incredible coincidence, or in a miracle-working God?

2. When my older daughter was six years old, she had disfiguring warts all over both hands. Shortly after she entered first grade, a doctor removed some of the warts, using an electric needle; all but one of them grew back. In addition to her concerns about her appearance, the warts actually made writing difficult. We all began to pray for them to be removed. We did not see any immediate results, but we kept praying. One morning, after about six weeks of regular prayer, my daughter came downstairs and said excitedly, "Look at my hands!" Every wart had disappeared completely; only one small scar remained from the wart that had not grown back after the earlier surgery. Now, over three decades later, her hands are still wart-free.

3. One summer afternoon in 1977, a wasp stung my wife. She very quickly began to feel dizzy and the right side of her face swelled severely, so she was rushed to a hospital. After administering an antihistamine, the doctor told her that she had developed a life-threatening allergy to wasp stings and that she should carry a dose of the antihistamine with her at all times, because otherwise the next sting would almost

certainly be fatal. Even after the medicine was administered, her face was swollen for days. The following year, she was stung again and was taken to the hospital. There, the treatment halted the progression of the swelling and dizziness, but did not reverse the symptoms. She was kept under observation for two hours, then sent home, feeling too weak to sit or stand, and too much in pain to lie down. Having recently been studying the miracles of the Bible, such as Paul's being bitten by a viper and having no ill effects (Acts 28:1-6), she decided to claim her healing by faith. At this point, her entire body was covered with welts and rash, the sense of burning made contact with the bed unbearably painful, and she still felt dizzy. But she began praying and soon fell asleep. When she awoke two hours later, her body was perfectly normal. She regained her strength much more rapidly than before, and the sting also healed quickly.

4. I was plowing my garden with my walking tractor one afternoon. As I was backing the tractor up, I inadvertently backed into a tree. When you back up a walking tractor, you have to lift the plow out of the ground and hold the tractor's handlebars up. The torque of the engine helps you to do this, since it tries to rotate the tractor in the opposite direction from the wheels. So I was stuck with my back to a tree and the tractor beginning to come back against me. Automatically, I pushed in the clutch. Without the engine's torque to hold the plow, the entire 150-lb weight of the tractor's back end and plow dropped from about a one-foot height and landed with the bottom of the steel plow across the small bones on the top of my left foot. I screamed for my older daughter, who was the only other person at home, and she helped me to hobble down to the house. I took off my sock and shoe and lay down, asking her to lay her hands on my foot and pray for healing. I went to work the next day, but left for a previously scheduled appointment with my doctor. I showed him the foot. When he saw the depth, color, and extent of the bruising, he said he was sure my foot was broken. Then he asked me to do several motions

with my foot and toes. Astonished that I completed them successfully, he told me that I could not have done those things with a broken foot, yet he had never seen an injury that looked like that not involve a fracture. He said there was nothing he could do to help. Within a week, I was walking without a limp.

5. (Betty Jane describes this next example in her own words.)
I stared in dismay at the paint cans before me. Eight one-gallon cans lay open at my feet, and twenty-one pairs of eyes were watching to see what I would do. We were gathered in a building being renovated for use as a Christian coffeehouse. Opening night was only two days away, and we were far behind schedule in our preparations.

Wednesday morning, sitting alone among the ladders and sawdust, I began to doubt whether we could pull it off. "God," I prayed, "we believe this coffeehouse is your idea, your plan. Please show me whether we should delay our opening."

Just then a slender, dark-haired man walked in the front door. Reverend Robert Kerr, pastor of Christ Chapel United Methodist Church, had heard of our efforts and agreed that the community needed such a facility. Asking about the status of the project, he learned of our quandary.
"Would it help if sixteen teenagers showed up tonight armed with paint rollers and trays?" he asked.
"Absolutely!" I exclaimed, my heart leaping with hope. "That would be a God-send."

Promising to return at 7:00 p.m. with his church youth group, Kerr left. Looking around, I realized how much cleaning up I had to do before the group arrived. All day I kept reminding myself that I should check the paint supply, in case I needed to purchase more, but always I decided something else needed to be done first. Now I stood with the group around me, my heart sinking, knowing there was nowhere to buy more paint at this hour. Everyone was waiting for me to tell them what to do.

There was a full gallon of blue that was too dark to go into a mix, but could be used alone. "Okay, let's break up the youth into teams of two. One team can take the blue and paint the office."

Bob Kerr quickly assigned partners and appointed the pair to start with the blue paint. Other adult volunteers moved a ladder into place for them and the painting began.

Surveying the remaining paint cans— a full gallon of ivory plus partial cans of white, yellow, and brown— I judged that we had enough light paint to offset the darkness of the small amount of brown. However, it all totaled only two and a half gallons, and we had sixteen hundred square feet of sheet rock to paint.

I had painted bare sheet rock before and knew how it drinks paint. Apologizing to the group for not having assured an adequate paint supply, I suggested we just do what we could. My friend Newell Davis helped me pour all the remaining paint into a five-gallon bucket, and we took turns stirring until the color was a uniform beige.

"Okay, we only have two more ladders. Let's have one team start at the front of each side wall and paint from chest height up. Another team can start at the back of each side wall, painting from chest height down. And be careful when you cross in the middle," I admonished. "One team on the stage, another in the canteen area. Last team paints the back hallway. We'll divide the paint evenly among the teams. Everybody keep going as long as you have paint, and we'll see where we stand afterward."

The group swung into action, and I assigned an adult volunteer to supervise each team. I was fighting back tears, realizing God had provided the manpower we needed, and I had failed Him by not providing adequate paint. I crossed the room to stand with Newell, gaining comfort from her presence.

Before long, the teams began reporting back. Each team had finished its assignment and had some paint left. I looked around in astonishment, questioning whether they had correctly understood my instructions. The adults confirmed that the entire room had received a coat of paint. When we poured all the little bits of paint back into the bucket, we still had a half gallon!

"That's impossible," I murmured. "Did we *really* cover sixteen hundred square feet of sheet rock with only two gallons of paint?"

"It's like fishes and loaves!" chuckled Newell.

"Okay, let's have just two teams divide the remaining paint. First look around for any spots that look thin and retouch them first. If you still have paint, just start at the front and go toward the back until you run out of paint."

Bob Kerr marshaled his forces and the painting proceeded, while the rest of us marveled aloud. Thirty minutes later, the entire room had a second coat of paint— and a few ounces of paint still remained!

6. After the coffeehouse opened, a young man came in one night just to hang around. We saw him again and again, and finally he told us his story. His father was an alcoholic, and so he had learned early to stay out of the house as much as possible. During high school, he became involved with tobacco, alcohol, and virtually all kinds of drugs. One evening when he was stoned, he began realizing just what a mess he had made of his life. He attended a church service, and when the altar call came, he felt moved to surrender his life to Jesus. He prayed for release from the drugs, and from

that day some thirty years ago until today, he has not had a cigarette, a drink of alcohol, or any other drug. He changed his entire set of friends, threw away all the phonograph records that represented his old life, and became very active in a new church. He has completed a college degree and owns his own successful decorating business. Often he will spend part or all of his vacation on mission in Mexico.

7. In the summer of 1989, my wife and I were in Haiti on a mission trip. While we were conducting a Bible school, we heard shouts from the road beside the church. A man had been hit by a passing truck and was bleeding severely. Help was needed to get him to the hospital at Port-Au-Prince, some eighteen miles away. Two nurses who were in our mission group grabbed their bags and ran to help. No stretcher was available, but someone brought the only substitute that could be found: a board that had been used to lay chickens' necks against as they were slaughtered. They took care to turn the nails downward before bundling the man onto it. Then a driver and two long-term missionaries from our group loaded the man into a van and left for the hospital. One of the nurses was monitoring vital signs as they drove. About five miles up the road, she announced quietly, "I have no pulse." The other nurse checked and agreed. Then one of the long-term missionaries ordered, "Quick, a prayer circle." They formed a circle and began to pray for the man as the first nurse continued to hold his wrist. The pulse came back strong. A week later, the man was released from the hospital with no long-term damage from his brush with death.

In addition to my own personal miraculous experiences here is another from a reliable witness.

One evening when Baptist teacher and minister Tony Campolo had just finished addressing an audience, a woman approached him, saying that God had told her to come to this place for her son to be healed. Both of the boy's legs were severely deformed, and he could not walk normally.

Doctors offered no hope. Dr. Campolo tried to explain that he couldn't heal her son, nor did he have any experience with faith-healing, and maybe she was supposed to go to a Pentecostal church. But she insisted. After a few minutes, the host pastor recalled the instructions in the Bible: "Is one of you ill? He should send for the elders of the congregation to pray over him and anoint him with oil in the name of the Lord. The prayer offered in faith will save the sick man, the Lord will raise him from his bed, and any sins he may have committed will be forgiven" (James 5:14-15, NEB). So they prayed and anointed the boy with cooking oil— it was all they could find. He left the building looking no better than when he came in. A year later, however, after Dr. Campolo had just finished a talk in that same city, the woman came walking down the aisle, accompanied by a bouncing, running boy.

"What happened?" Dr. Campolo asked.

"Don't you remember? You prayed for him," came the answer.

Dr. Campolo left the building that day awed by the power of God that had expressed itself because of the woman's faith, in spite of his own unbelief.

There are few forums in contemporary America for sharing stories of the miraculous. Two of the most reliable are *Guideposts* and *Believer's Voice of Victory* magazines. Even though not every story between their covers is about miracles, many are, and Christian people all over the world benefit from reading them. A few churches provide ways for members to share their special experiences with each other, and these are a tremendous help also. Unfortunately, the tradition of "testifying" in church has sometimes led people to feel a need to share something, even if it is fictional. A friend of mine calls these services in his former church "testilying services"! So we must maintain a delicate balance between providing an opportunity for sharing and providing a motivation for fabrication. Perhaps the key is that real sharing is possible only when there is a deep element of trust among the members of the church or group. For this reason, small prayer groups and mission-study groups sometimes serve this function better than an entire church can.

The Laws of Faith

Altogether too many Christians feel quite comfortable talking about faith in the context of ultimate salvation, but become very fidgety when miracles are brought up. They believe that God can heal, but they silently believe He has to do so through an M.D. They have faith that God can bless them financially, but they secretly think that He must do so through their job, or the lottery, or some other established (and expected) channel. Receptiveness to miracles somehow has been identified with pagan superstition. Miracles are a stumbling-block to too many Christians today.

Just what is a miracle? Numerous definitions have been given, many of them prejudicial.[10] *Webster's Encyclopedic Unabridged Dictionary* says a miracle is "an effect or extraordinary event in the physical world which surpasses all known human or natural powers and is ascribed to a supernatural cause". Since a dictionary simply records usage, we can accept this definition as theologically neutral. In *Miracles*, C. S. Lewis proposes that we consider miracles to be an intrusion of God into our ordinary world, breaking the laws of physics in the process. This is a peculiar idea for Lewis, since in the novel *That Hideous Strength* he has the following conversation between the skeptical Scot, MacPhee, the physician Grace Ironwood, and professors Dimble and Denniston concerning a condition that appears miraculous:

---

[10]If I am asked to define *anchovy*, and I respond by saying it's an overwhelmingly oversalted small nasty fish sometimes used to ruin pizza, I have given a definition that prejudices all attempts to discuss the anchovy objectively. Similarly, if I define *miracle* as an event designed to inspire faith, I have injected so much interpretation into the definition that we can no longer meaningfully discuss miracles. Unfortunately, such definitions abound in inspirational literature.

"All this has the disadvantage of being clean contrary to the observed laws of nature," observed MacPhee....

"It is not contrary to the laws of nature," said a voice from the corner where Grace Ironwood sat, almost invisible in the shadows. "You are quite right. The laws of the universe are never broken. Your mistake is to think that the little regularities we have observed on one planet for a few hundred years are the real unbreakable laws; whereas they are only the remote results which the true laws bring about more often than not; as a kind of accident."

After further discussion, MacPhee brings out his heavy armaments:

"Not many exceptions to the law of death have come my way," observed MacPhee.

"And *how*," said Grace with much emphasis, "how should *you* expect to be there on more than one such occasion?... Did you know Enoch or Elijah?"[11]

In fact, we are always expanding our knowledge of the physical world. When Isaac Newton published the *Principia Mathematica* in 1687, he established the basis for mechanical physics. But upon publication of his General Theory of Relativity, Albert Einstein identified Newton's physics as one special case that applies under the conditions in which we usually live. Under other conditions, such as at extremely high velocities, Newton's understanding is incomplete. Dozens of other examples could be given. It is egotistical to assume that at any point in time we have a complete scientific knowledge in any field. Therefore, to say that the miraculous represents God breaking His own laws makes little sense. Notice that Webster's dictionary only claims that the miracle surpasses all **known** human or natural powers. This leaves open the possibility that a miracle is an occurrence that makes use of laws that we do not yet understand.

---

[11]C. S. Lewis; *That Hideous Strength*, (New York: Macmillan, 1965). 367-368.

Of course the orderliness of this understanding appeals to me, because I believe that the working of physical law is God's way of keeping the universe running. But more importantly, it can open our eyes to experiences that we would have considered impossible. In *Beyond Biofeedback*, Drs. Elmer and Alice Green, formerly of the Menninger Institute, describe clinical demonstrations by a yogi in which he pierced his own arm with a knitting needle, then withdrew it with immediate spontaneous wound closure and only one small drop of blood. This kind of control over the autonomic nervous system might seem miraculous, but in reality it is an example of mental practice producing physical results. Persons trained using biofeedback have learned to produce the same "miraculous" results. We are beginning to glimpse the workings of the laws of the mind in ways that may still seem unbelievable. It seems reasonable to me that Jesus was able to perform miracles by the workings of these and other laws which we do not yet understand. I find it rather egotistical to say that God can perform miracles only by setting aside natural law. Doing so claims far too much for the meager state of our knowledge of natural law.

In fact, many of the principles discussed in this book are means for fostering the miraculous. Jesus Himself gave us the key in His many teachings on faith. And Paul made it clear that miracles are not peripheral to Christianity, but are integral parts of our faith. "The kingdom of God is not a matter of talk, but of power." (1 Corinthians 4:20, NEB) If we look carefully into the Scriptures, we can find seven laws for activating faith in our lives.

Law 1: Know God
As this book has mentioned more than once, we have faith in a Person, not an event or desired result. To have genuine faith in any person, we have to know that person. Scripture study and daily communion are the two best ways to know God more fully. We don't have to know *how* God works, only that He *will* work in our lives.

As we grow in our knowledge of the Person and character of God, we will also grow in our understanding of His will. This understanding is essential to our faith.

Law 2: Practice your faith.

The first aspect of practicing faith is simply choosing faith instead of fear. Most of our acquaintances come down on the wrong side of this choice most of the time. Stop before you say, "Well, I planted my garden on time this year, but just you wait; we'll have a storm or a drought or something." Instead say, "Well, I planted my garden on time this year, and I'm looking forward to some great tomatoes and corn pretty soon!" There's nothing complicated about speaking our positive expectations rather than living in negativity, but it is difficult. So much of our social conversation revolves around making grim half-jokes about how bad things are, or soon will be. Jesus said that we can have what we say. It makes sense, then, to say what we want. (Or in psychological terms, we should keep our mouths' suggestions to our subconscious minds in line with our conscious desires.)

The other aspect of practicing faith is to act upon our beliefs. Certainly prayer is part of this action. Seeing the answer in our minds is another part. If I wake up with a sniffle and decide that I'm getting a cold, then go back to bed, I'll likely develop a cold. I have seen the runny nose and general discomfort mentally. But if I remember that God's will is for my health, and tell myself that I choose not to develop a cold that would be contrary to His will, then I can mentally picture myself in the bloom of health, and I can experience that health instead of the cold.

Many well-meaning Christians object to this line of thought by saying, "Well old Mrs. Grisbourne was as fine a Christian as I ever knew, and she had colds all the time." If Mrs. Grisbourne had never plugged in her electric toaster, she would have eaten soft bread for breakfast, too. Yes, she showed her faith by her Christian works, but did she apply it to her health? Making the specific application of faith is like plugging in the toaster; results depend on this step. Unless we ask for something specific, believing that we have received it when we ask, then we have not used our faith.

Law 3: Be Real

Do not draw artificial distinctions between "spiritual" and "physical" means, for "the LORD your God is One." The barrier we often place between our professed beliefs and our everyday lives is an enemy to faith. People often ask, "Does faith in God's will require that I give up human help?" The question may refer to the use of doctors for help in healing, the use of financial advisors for help with one's bills or investments, or any other perceived conflicts between the "spiritual" and the "physical". Going back to the example of the early-morning sniffle, there is absolutely nothing contrary to faith in my drinking extra orange juice, since it will aid my natural resistance. In doing so, I am helping the manifestation of God's will for my health. Certainly God does not *need* the orange juice to keep me from getting a cold. But then Jesus said that doing the Father's will was food and drink to him (John 4:34), yet he usually ate and drank like any other human. If I feel that I am doing my part to take care of my body (the temple) by drinking the juice, then I should do so.

Going further, if I knowingly or unwittingly allow the sniffle to become a cold, applying physical remedies is not contrary to faith. But if I transfer my confidence in God's healing power to anything else— a pill, a person, or anything— then I have wavered in my faith and cannot expect the Lord to give me anything (James 1:8). In other words, as soon as I start thinking, "If this faith stuff doesn't work, I can just go to the doctor," I have set up a barrier to the action of my faith.

Law 4: Speak Your Beliefs Aloud.

As we hear our own mouths proclaiming our faith, that faith is strengthened. This is usually better done in private; else, we find ourselves fighting the unbelief of others! Conversely, as we refuse to speak contrary to our faith, whether in public or in private, our faith grows.

Law 5: Don't dig up the seed.

> The kingdom of God is like this. A man scatters seed on the land; he goes to bed at night and gets up in the morning, and the seed sprouts and

grows—how, he does not know. The ground produces a crop by itself, first the blade, then the ear, then the full-grown corn in the ear; but as soon as the crop is ripe, he plies the sickle, because harvest-time has come. (Mark 4:26-29, NEB)

The farmer who plants his seed and then goes and digs it up to see if it is growing will never have a crop. The Christian who worries the object of his request—"watching the pot," to use another metaphor—will likely be disappointed. The farmer who has faith in the processes of nature, even though he does not understand them, will reap the harvest. The Christian who asks in faith, believing, then goes on about his business, will receive.

Here is another paradox: Jesus said to keep on praying and not give up (Matthew 18:1), but we see that continuing to make the same petition is digging up the seed and shows lack of faith. The key to this paradox is the way we pray. When we have prayed for a significant miracle, that request naturally comes to mind in subsequent prayers. However, we do not need to ask again. Instead, we can pause and visualize the prayer answered, then thank God for His answer. In that way we keep on praying and do not give up, but we do so in faith.

Law 6: Stay positive.

Even worse than digging up the seed is sprinkling it with herbicide. Negativity is herbicide to faith. We've already discussed keeping our thoughts and words positive. But we must also avoid negativity from others, insofar as possible. Jesus often sent away even the friends and family of people he was going to heal, allowing only the faithful disciples to attend. Even Jesus could not perform mighty works in the presence of great negativity (see Matthew 13: 53-58).

After the results of our prayer of faith are securely manifested, we may then share "praise reports" with others. Be aware that Christians, perhaps even more than non-Christians, will often try to argue you out of your belief. There are recorded cases of people who experienced "spontaneous cures" from cancer (medical terminology for a miracle) who went back into family situations brandishing favorable doctors' reports, only to succumb to the unbelief of their families. In a misguided effort to keep the former patient from "getting his hopes up," these loved ones torpedoed that life-saving faith, and the patient relapsed, dying as they all had expected. ("As thou hast believed, so be it done unto thee" [Matthew 8:13, KJV].) Since hope is the blueprint, keeping a patient from "getting his hopes up" takes away the blueprint for his faith to act upon.

Always pray for guidance before sharing the results of your faith. Praise reports can be powerful agents for good when given to appropriate people at appropriate times. But they can unintentionally breed strife when they are used inappropriately.

Law 7: Get on with your life.

Hold your faith in peace, not in mental exertion. Don't brood or let any issue paralyze you. If I ask my lawyer to prepare a will for me, I then go on my way knowing that the matter is taken care of. I don't need to wear myself out "believing" that he is preparing the will. Surely I can have at least that much faith in God!

Often Christians are encouraged to "see the answer" as they pray. If this means my prayer for career success is accompanied by a mental image of myself feeling happy and fulfilled, secure in the knowledge that I am doing God's will, then all is well. But if it means that I see myself in a particular job or office, or drawing a particular salary, then my mental image limits God's response to my prayer of faith. It is vital that I let God be God, choosing what He knows is best for me, not what I may think is best. Certainly He wills career success for me, but He may well define it differently than I do.

It is equally vital that those of us (myself included) who do not easily construct visual mental images not feel as if we fail in faith because we do not "see the answer". I experience faith more often as a feeling of peace, knowing that I have turned my problem over to a loving Daddy. Mental imagery is a valuable tool for those who can use it, but each person must experience and express faith in his or her own way.

Preparation for Prayer

I t may seem strange to find a chapter on preparation near the end
of a book rather than at the beginning. But to understand
preparation for prayer, we needed discussions that have come
earlier in this book.

Jesus gave us several specific instructions on prayer, and he acted out
a few more. Those will be our focus in this chapter.

> Again, when you pray, do not be like the
> hypocrites; they love to say their prayers standing
> up in the synagogue and at the street corners, for
> everyone to see them. I tell you this: they have
> their reward already. But when you pray, go into
> a room by yourself, shut the door, and pray to
> your Father who is there in the secret place; and
> your Father who sees what is secret will reward
> you.
> (Matthew 6:5-6, NEB)

The word *hypocrite* comes from the Greek *hypokrités*, meaning "actor"
(literally, "under greasepaint"). When actors perform, they "play to
the audience". The reward for the performance is the applause, the
congratulations of fellow-actors, and perhaps favorable press reviews.
There are religious actors. These people go into prayer with the same
motivations as the secular actors have. Jesus tells us that their prayers
are answered— not necessarily their spoken prayers, but the prayers
of their hearts, which are for public recognition.

As Christians, we set our sights far higher when we pray: we seek to
commune (become one with) the Most High! Jesus says that to do
this, we must pray alone. How do we reconcile this with Matthew

18:20, where Jesus tells us that He is in the midst of any two or three who are gathered in His name? First, we must recognize that we are discussing different kinds of prayer. In Matthew 6, Jesus is discussing the prayer of communion, visiting with Daddy, meditating, if you will. This is the prayer that underlies all others. Without relationship and communion, we cannot count on our prayer petitions being in accord with God's will, and consequently we cannot be assured that the petitions will be answered. In Matthew 18, the focus is on believers acting together as the Body of Christ. In order to function in this way, we must first cultivate a close relationship with the Father. This must be done one-on-one. The reward is the closer relationship that we were seeking.

The subject of surroundings was touched upon in the chapter on meditation. It is easier to focus on God when we are in an appropriate physical location. Jesus said that when we pray, we should go into a closet. (KJV) Now if you have a closet that fosters an attitude of oneness with God, by all means pray in it! My closets would require hours of excavation before I could even get inside to pray. And then I would probably feel uncomfortable and stifled. What Jesus is saying here is that we should remove ourselves from the distractions of the world.

> Randall went to a state-supported college located in a mountain town. Having grown up in a small-town church, he now found himself in very secular surroundings. It was easiest to use Sundays to catch up on badly needed rest. When he went to one of the local churches, he felt awkward and out of place. (Had he known it, his story was that of most young collegians!) Then one weekend he made a trip to a nearby national forest with some friends. They decided to have a picnic on the flat top of a mountain that overlooked a waterfall. The fall leaves framing the distant waterfall made an entrancing, almost hypnotic vista. Suddenly, he felt The Presence. The God that he thought he had left at home, and had failed to find in the college-town churches, was here on the mountain top. With his friends having gone back to the car for the food, the vastness of the mountains had become Randall's closet. He was alone less

than five minutes, but during those minutes time stood still, and when the friends returned, he felt as though he had been washed in love for an eternity. Years later, Randall still develops a catch in his throat when he talks of the experience. And when he needs to get away from the world, he goes back to this same place where the surroundings seem to bring him closer to God.

Peter Marshall, the great Scottish-born preacher of a few decades ago, found his closet at the beach. Whether walking along the sand, or rowing about in a small boat, he often heard his Father speak most clearly when he was near the seashore. On the other hand, Helmut Thielicke and Dietrich Bonhoeffer closeted themselves with God inside German prisons. Jesus went to the mountains to pray (Luke 6:15, 9:28). The place doesn't matter. The ability to feel alone with God matters very much.

After the destruction of the Temple and most of Jerusalem in 587 BC, many of the people of God were deported to Babylon. Having a centuries-old heritage that located God in the Temple, they were spiritually crushed.

> By the rivers of Babylon we sat down and wept
>   when we remembered Zion.
> There on the willow-trees
>   we hung up our harps,
> for there those who carried us off
>   demanded music and singing,
> and our captors called on us to be merry:
>   "Sing us one of the songs of Zion."
> How could we sing the LORD's song
>   in a foreign land?
> (Psalm 137:1-4, NEB)

One of the great lessons of the exile was that Yahweh is not limited by buildings or cities or even national boundaries. We too must learn this lesson. Beautiful mountain scenes may help us to meet God, but God is not limited to the mountain. His still, small voice can speak to us anywhere that we choose to be alone with Him and listen. Jesus's recommendation of a closet for prayer was intended to help us, not to serve as a rule. While helpful, it must not become a chain.

All of us have seen paintings of small children praying on their knees at their bedsides. In some movies we see a rebellious character ultimately submitting to God by kneeling in prayer. Certainly kneeling is a valid prayer position, and sometimes it feels like the best one. But contrary to ideas that some of us may have absorbed, it is not the only good position. In Mark 11:25, Jesus said, "when you stand praying, if you have a grievance against anyone, forgive him, so that your Father in heaven may forgive the wrongs you have done" (NEB). In Gethsemane, our Lord "fell on his face in prayer, and said, 'My Father, if it is possible, let this cup pass me by. Yet not as I will, but as thou wilt'" (Matthew 26:39, NEB). I think that the point is that our physical position in prayer is not important. Any position that helps express our genuine feeling toward our Father is valid. After all, how many of us spend a lot of time planning our physical position before we address our earthly father?

Though not specifically commanded in the Bible, fasting is a very effective means of preparing for prayer. Let's try to put this ancient practice into perspective. When you have just eaten to the fill, how do you feel? From my vast experience with church picnics, I can answer with authority that the feeling is one of a pleasant dullness and lethargy. I am not a particularly good listener when I am stuffed. I may fall asleep in the middle of your sentence! One Christian teacher was discussing the common practice of churches when they bring in a guest preacher. In order to make him or her feel welcome, prominent members often invite the guest for prayer breakfasts, luncheon meetings, and dinner parties. Given this custom, the teacher asked, is it any wonder that sometimes we hear more turkey than Word from our preachers? Certainly, right after a full meal is not a good time for prayer.

However, to most twenty-first-century Christians, fasting seems a little extreme. We all know what fasting is: you don't eat and then you get very hungry. Somehow that is supposed to impress God because you bear the hunger pangs. Why should God be impressed by this? I have been asked variants of this question by literally dozens of

Christians, young and old. Let me say right up front that if all you expect when you fast is to get very hungry, you will not be disappointed. But to understand the purpose and practice of fasting more fully, we first have to examine some of our own cultural history.

The thrust of the Bible makes it clear that we are spirits; we have souls, and we live in bodies. Jesus said, "The spirit it is that giveth life— The flesh profiteth nothing" (John 6:63a, Rhm). The Old-Testament Hebrews never really understood this, nor do most modern Christians. We are like children in bumper-cars at a carnival. Very soon after a child starts driving a bumper-car, the child begins expressing his or her personality through the car. Aggressive children will push each other around, sometimes viciously. Children who are not assertive may well not enjoy the bumper-cars at all, because they will just provide another opportunity for them to be pushed around. Since for all of our earthly lives we have lived in bodies, we express ourselves through them, and they become an extension of our personalities just as the bumper-cars do for the kids. Of course the difference is that a child in a bumper-car can see his hands and feet, so he does not forget about his body. But we cannot see our spirits or our souls, and so we can forget about them, and come to identify with our bodies. The error is easy to understand, but just as easy to expose. My friend Annie is 93 years old, but she has the creativity, spontaneity, vivacity, and sense of humor of a teenager, coupled with the mental and emotional seasoning of a long life. To identify Annie with her 93-year-old body is simply logically impossible. Other cases could be named, including those with physical handicaps, such as physicist Stephen Hawking.

For millennia, people believed in the spirit world, although they had little understanding of it. All human-made religions bear witness to this fact. But with the Age of Enlightenment (1600-1800), we began to develop some scientific understanding of invisible things such as gravity and wind and wave motion. These no longer had to be explained by direct spiritual intervention. So we collectively abandoned any idea of spiritual reality wholesale, throwing out the baby with the bathwater. Most modern materialists are still bound by this same spiritual darkness, thinking themselves sophisticated and clever. In fact, science itself cannot support a materialistic world view, nor has it been able to since the middle 1800's, if one evaluates the evidence dispassionately. Those who call upon science to support their materialism are about a century and a half out of date!

If we confine our attention to the question of scientific support for materialism, we can fairly restate that question as, "Does modern science satisfactorily explain all observed phenomena without the intrusion of a non-material reality?" In answer to this question, we first observe that according to the Copenhagen interpretation of quantum physics, explanation of how or why quantum events occur may not be within the scope of that science; the purpose of the science is only to predict what will occur under given circumstances. For an excellent discussion of the vast gaps in understanding that exist within quantum physics, look at *The Dancing Wu Li Masters*, by Gary Zukov. Next, we look at so-called psychic phenomena, including telepathy, clairvoyance, clairaudience, pre- and retro-cognition, and telekinesis. The reality of all these phenomena has been proven in numerous laboratories world-wide, and results have been reported in well-respected peer-reviewed scientific journals. In fact clairvoyance has been used militarily by the US Army (Project Stargate, declassified in the mid-1990's). Attempts to fit these occurrences into the present understanding of science have met with no success. For more information, read *Psychic Exploration*, by Astronaut Dr. Edwin Mitchell; and *Science and Human Transformation*, by internationally respected physicist Dr. William Tiller. For specific examples of research reported in mainstream scientific journals, supporting the efficacy of prayer, see *Healing Words* and *Prayer Is Good* Medicine, by Larry Dossey, M.D. Other examples of the failure of science to support materialism abound.

But lest we digress, the point is that though we may have forgotten it, we are basically spiritual beings who express through our bodies so fully that in a sense, we become one with them. True spiritual growth necessarily involves manifesting the spiritual dimension more fully. "God is spirit, and those who worship him must worship in spirit and in truth" (John 4:24, NEB). The entire purpose of fasting is to enable us to worship and commune with the Father in spirit. This occurs because of a complex set of physiological reactions that occur after we have fasted for a time. The specific effects could be explained more fully by an endocrinologist or neurologist, but in laymen's terms, there are three stages of fasting. In the first stage, we feel hunger and may become weak, perhaps dizzy. This passes after a day or so, as the body re-programs itself to exist on stored food. The second stage is characterized by a feeling that is perhaps best described as detachment, in which we feel intensely alert and alive, but not entirely concerned or involved with the things that are going on around us. In this stage, meditation is usually a much deeper and more dramatic experience. The physiological condition of our body is such that normal waking consciousness is transformed into a sort of reverie state. This is similar to the state just before we fall asleep at night. It is neither wise nor safe to drive, operate machinery, or engage in heavy exercise during this stage of fasting.

The third stage is one that we will seldom enter, as it only comes after a very extended time. This is when the body has exhausted its stores of fat and begins to digest muscle for the calories needed to sustain metabolism. It is described in the Bible:

> Full of the Holy Spirit, Jesus returned from the Jordan, and for forty days was led by the Spirit up and down the wilderness and tempted by the devil. All that time he had nothing to eat, and at the end of it he was famished.
> (Luke 4:1-2, NEB)

At this stage, the body is close to starvation, and fasting must be ended. Normally, about a three-week fast would be needed to enter this stage. But since stage two is the one that promotes our meditation and communion with the Father, we really don't need to try to attain stage three. Usually a two- or three-day fast is the most we need to undertake.

Christians who are uncomfortable with fasting often point out Jesus's response to the disciples of John the Baptizer:

> Then John's disciples came to him with the question: "Why do we and the Pharisees fast, but

your disciples do not?" Jesus replied, "Can you
expect the bridegroom's friends to go mourning
while the bridegroom is with them? The time will
come when the bridegroom will be taken away
from them; that will be the time for them to
fast."
(Matthew 9:14-15, NEB)

This is a very obscure answer. Notice that this event occurs before
the arrest of John, so it is relatively early in Jesus's ministry. The first
time that Jesus openly told anyone that He was the Messiah was in
the encounter with the Samaritan woman some time later, and even
then He did not openly claim to be the Son of God. He verified
Peter's revelation of His identity, but that was later also, and was not
mentioned to any but the disciples. I believe that when John's
disciples questioned Jesus about fasting, He answered them on their
own level. They were not ready to understand that He was the Son of
God, and that just being with Him met much of the purpose of
fasting for His disciples. And since in this text Jesus identified fasting
with mourning, it is quite likely that John's disciples did not even
understand the real purpose of fasting anyway, but considered it to
be a sort of penance for sins.

It is clear from other texts that Jesus expected the disciples to fast,
though not perhaps as John's disciples understood fasting. As we've
already mentioned, Jesus fasted before the temptation in the
wilderness. That fast seems to have been for the purpose of gaining
spiritual guidance and clarification concerning His entire ministry.
During the Sermon on the Mount, Jesus taught His disciples:

> So too when you fast, do not look gloomy like
> the hypocrites: they make their faces unsightly so
> that other people may see that they are fasting. I
> tell you this: they have their reward already. But
> when you fast, anoint your head and wash your
> face, so that men may not see that you are
> fasting, but only your Father who is in the secret
> place, and your Father who sees what is in secret
> will give you your reward.
> (Matthew 6:16-18, NEB)

Notice that He said, "*when* you fast", not "*if* you fast". Fasting was
assumed. But the fasting was not of a kind that the disciples of John
would have noticed. As we noted, Jesus equated their kind of fasting
with mourning, which certainly is related to looking "gloomy like the
hypocrites".

Fasting was also practiced in the early church.

> There were at Antioch, in the congregation there,
> certain prophets and teachers: Barnabas, Simeon
> called Niger, Lucius of Cyrene, Manaen, who had
> been at the court of Prince Herod, and Saul.
> While they were keeping a fast and offering
> worship to the Lord, the Holy Spirit said, "Set
> Barnabas and Saul apart for me, to do the work
> for which I have called them." Then, after
> further fasting and prayer, they laid their hands
> on them and let them go.
> (Acts 13:1-3, NEB)

Notice several things:

- Fasting was associated with worship, not with penance.
- Fasting seemed to be associated with receiving guidance from God.
- Even after the guidance had been received, the fasting and prayer were continued, perhaps for further guidance,

clarification, and empowerment preparatory to laying on of hands.

According to ancient records, baptism in the early church was associated with fasting. In keeping with the example of John and Jesus, baptism was given to adults who had made a personal decision to commit their lives to Jesus. Baptismal candidates would begin fasting on Good Friday evening, and would devote all Saturday to fasting and prayer. Then early on Easter morning, the congregation leader would come forward in white robes and take the blindfolded candidates one by one into the baptismal river. As they rose from the water, the blindfold was removed and their eyes were bathed in the first light of morning. The gathered congregation would then take communion, the first for the new converts, and offer hymns of praise. (These same converts were among those who chose to be thrown to wild beasts or burned alive rather than renounce their faith. I wonder how many of today's Christians, children of cheap decisions and easy baptisms, would even claim their faith if it were illegal, much less hold to it in the face of such terrors!)

There is no direct scriptural guidance as to when and how often to fast, or preparations for fasting. But I can offer some guidelines based on personal experience. Fasting should be done only in response to an inner prompting: if you feel led to fast, do so. A call to fast is often associated with a felt need for God's guidance on a particular matter, or just a need to feel more closely attuned to God. Time your fasting when you can devote some time to meditating and visiting with our Father. A fast squeezed into the middle of earthly concerns is seldom of any use. Prepare for your fast by avoiding caffeine, alcohol, and excess sugar for at least a couple of weeks. Faced with severe headaches every time he fasted, a friend asked a physician how he could avoid them. According to the doctor, traces of caffeine and other drosses produced by the body from alcohol or excess sugar can be stored with fat, and when the body calls upon stored fats to meet energy needs during fasting, these physiological pollutants also enter the bloodstream and cause headaches. Whether the explanation is medically correct or not, avoiding these substances does significantly reduce fast-related (and even non-fast-related) headaches.

Fasting does not usually include doing without liquids. In fact, a person fasting needs to pay particular attention to drinking the normal amount of water. A modification of a total food fast is a juice fast, in which fruit juice is substituted for part of the water. This is a milder form of fast than a total food fast, both in terms of physical stress and psychophysiological results.

Not all fasts even involve food. Isaiah poetically records a conversation between God and Israel that not only exposes their "pre-Pharisaic" ideas of fasting, but introduces some new ideas on the subject:

[The People]
        Why do we fast, if thou dost not see it?
        Why mortify ourselves, if thou payest no heed?
[God]
        Since you serve your own interest only on your
        fast-day
          and make your men work all the harder,
     since your fasting leads only to wrangling and
     strife
          and dealing vicious blows with the fist,
          on such a day you are keeping no fast
          that will carry your cry to heaven.
     Is it a fast like this that I require,
          a day of mortification such as this,
          that a man should bow his head like a bulrush
          and make his bed on sackcloth and ashes?
          Is this what you call a fast,
           a day acceptable to the LORD?
     Is not this what I require of you as a fast:
          to loose the fetters of injustice,
          to untie the knots of the yoke,
          to snap every yoke
          and set free those who have been crushed?
     Is it not sharing your food with the hungry,
     taking the homeless poor into your house,
          clothing the naked when you meet them

and never evading a duty to your kinsfolk?
(Isaiah 58:3-7, NEB)

Notice that the people begin with the assumption that fasting is only a ritual engaged for the purpose of impressing God. They do not understand that fellowship with God, and being blessed by God, require living in ways that God can acknowledge and bless. In His response, their Father tries to move them into a fuller understanding. Those who fast their time, using it instead to fight injustice and bondage; those who fast their bounty, feeding and clothing the hungry; those who fast their privacy, sharing their homes with the homeless; those who fast their independence, giving their help to their kinsfolk— these are the ones who will experience fellowship with their Daddy and be blessed by the Most High.

Jesus said the same thing almost six hundred years after Isaiah:

> When the Son of Man comes in his glory and all the angels with him, he will sit in state on his throne, with all the nations gathered before him. He will separate men into two groups, as a shepherd separates the sheep from the goats, and he will place the sheep on his right hand and the goats on his left. Then the king will say to those on his right hand, "You have my Father's blessing; come, enter and possess the kingdom that has been ready for you since the world was made. For when I was hungry, you gave me food; when thirsty, you gave me drink; when I was a stranger you took me into your home, when naked you clothed me; when I was ill you came to my help, when in prison you visited me." Then the righteous will reply, "Lord, when was it that we saw you hungry and fed you, or thirsty and gave you drink, a stranger and took you home, or naked and clothed you? When did we see you ill or in prison, and come to visit you?" And the king will answer, "I tell you this:

anything you did for one of my brothers here, however humble, you did for me."
(Matthew 25:31-40, NEB)

Professor John Carlton taught at Southeastern Baptist Theological Seminary. One cold day, he was in his office visiting with a student named Pennington. They had just discussed the professor's beautiful new overcoat when a foreign exchange student entered to ask a question. After answering the question, Professor Carlton asked, "Aren't you cold?" The foreign student said yes, but explained that since the climate in his country was warm, he did not own a coat. "Then try this one," the professor invited. "I have others." The new coat was a perfect fit, and the student left feeling warmer in more than one way. Before he too left the office, Pennington invited Dr. Carlton for supper. "What time?" the professor asked. "Six o'clock," responded Pennington. "Fine," said Dr. Carlton. "That gives me time to run some errands in Raleigh... I've got to buy a coat."[12]

We may choose to fast material things for communion with God, or we may fast food as Jesus did for guidance, but ultimately living in fellowship with God comes down to living in God's way. And that is the subject of the next chapter.

---

[12]John I. Durham, ed., *Worship Beyond the Usual. An Echo of the Voice of John W. Carlton*, (Macon, GA: Mercer University Press, 1993), xv.

Contemporary Holiness

Hallow yourselves and be holy, because I the LORD your God am Holy.
(Leviticus 20:7, NEB)

We have discussed the fact that *holy* means "set apart for a specific purpose". As Christians, we are to be holy, just as the ancient Hebrews were commanded to be holy. But we have an immense advantage over them. The next verse in Leviticus 20 says, "You shall keep my rules and obey them: I am the LORD who hallows you" (Leviticus 20:8, NEB). The rules— the Law— are all the Hebrews had to go by. We have not only the example of the Christ, but the indwelling Holy Spirit to guide us. And yet not many of us are very holy. How can we find out what is lacking?

A profound, and profoundly necessary step in every person's spiritual growth is to carefully examine just what it is that we idealize. One way to do this is to remove oneself from the everyday distractions and then make a list of adjectives that apply to the very best person and friend we can imagine. All sorts of words may come to mind, such as *strong, creative, loving, fair*, etc. Be very honest with yourself. If adjectives such as *beautiful* and *rich* are a part of your ideal, list them too. Now while looking at this list, select the one that seems to best encapsulate all the others. This adjective represents your ideal, the core of what you really worship. The others fill out the description.

Although this exercise sounds simple, it is actually one of the most difficult bits of self-searching I have ever done. The problem is remaining honest with myself. We all know what things we *ought* to admire most in a person. The temptation is to list these attributes as our ideals. But then we consider the people we really do admire, and we often find that they are flashy celebrities rather than those who more fully live the quiet spiritual life. We are attracted by looks, wealth, physical strength, and witty personalities. But it gets worse. In fact, it is seldom the real celebrity we admire, but rather our romanticized image of that celebrity. Now we must choose between qualities we know we should admire and those that we actually prize most highly. However, this dilemma itself is a growing experience. As we begin to see the shallowness of some of our own preferences, we can begin to act as people whose "perceptions are trained by long use to discern good and evil" (Hebrews 5:14b, NEB).

There are several useful tests to help us gauge our honesty in identifying our ideal. One is to look at your check book for the past month. Categorize your expenditures: physical needs (food, clothing, shelter, health care, transportation and work-related expenses); gifts of relationship (birthday present for your brother); entertainment (movies, concerts, restaurants-for-fun, sports, boats); savings; and good works (gifts to the church, charity, missions support). Next, read Leviticus 27:30 and Matthew 23:23. Notice that Jesus said that the tithes should not be neglected. Read Matthew 25:31-45, and notice that the reward or condemnation was issued based upon what the people did or didn't *do*. Think about the fact that a number of organizations can feed and educate a third-world child for about twenty-eight dollars a month. How do your financial actions compare with the values you said you hold?

> Jessica lives alone and works as a nurse. Of her $3200 monthly salary, she takes home about $2400. Her apartment, car, and food cost $1350, and other physical needs bring the total to $1700. Gifts of relationship average $50 per month; entertainment is about $300; savings, $175; and good works, $175.

> Alan is a schoolteacher. His wife Jan works half-time as an insurance consultant. Between them they bring in a monthly take-home pay of about $3250. Physical needs for their family of five consume about $2750. Gifts of relationship average $70 each month; entertainment, $200; savings, $100, and good works, $130.

Of course we don't know Jessica, or Alan and Jan. But we can make a few observations. Jessica alone spends more on entertainment than do Alan and Jan's whole family. Is this irresponsible of her? Perhaps not. Living alone, Jessica must deal with loneliness, and the job of a nurse can be quite stressful. Perhaps her higher entertainment expenses are legitimate for meeting her emotional needs. On the other hand, perhaps she could also meet those needs by working with her church's youth group or a mission circle.

Neither Jessica, nor Alan and Jan save 10% of their take-home pay, as some financial advisors recommend. Neither do they tithe. But do they have enough income to do these things? Let me tell you a true story-within-a-story.

> Alton worked for a large electronics manufacturer, making an above-average salary. After several years, he decided to quit and go into business for himself. He and his family took an immediate 40% cut in income. But they had planned ways in which they could cut spending, and they found to their surprise that the money ran out about three days before the end of the month, just as it had always done at the higher salary. During this time, Alton and his wife Eve often had to work long hours at the business, so they sometimes hired Althea to help with the children. Althea, now in her sixties, had spent her life loving and caring for children. Her husband contributed almost no income. Therefore, although she was retirement age, her Social Security and earnings combined only barely covered her subsistence. (She did give $20 per month to her church!) One Thursday evening when Eve was driving Althea home, she asked whether Althea had enough money to cover her needs. "Oh, I'm just fine," she answered. "I've got Sunday dinner in the fridge. I ain't got nothing to worry 'bout." The perspective of three days' food constituting security was new to Eve!
>
> After several years, Alton's new business failed, and he began supporting his family day-to-day by doing electronic repairs. Some days at 4:00 P.M. it was not yet clear where supper was coming from. It was then that Alton and Eve learned (and began to teach their children) Althea's secret:

our basic needs are not really as great as we usually think they are.

Ed and Janet had been married for several years before they decided to return to church after the typical American collegiate hiatus. During the time away from church, they had done much searching, rediscovering a belief in God. Both had been taught as children the importance of tithing. But both had grown up in churches in which tithers were a distinct minority. One day the question of tithing came up, and both Ed and Janet felt led to commit to doing it. However, they found that there simply was not enough money left after they paid their bills. Then one month they decided to experiment. They wrote the tithe check first, then paid the other bills. The money seemed to go just as far then as before they began tithing. And they have tithed ever since.

Certainly each person and each family must identify its own financial priorities. But perhaps the stories of Jessica, Alan and Jan, Alton and Eve, Ed and Janet, and Althea will expand our vision. The point is this: there are clear instructions in Scripture about giving. Although the question of the purpose of the tithe is complex (see, for example, Numbers 18:21-24 and Deuteronomy 12:4-12, 14:22-29), Scripture leaves no question about God's intention that we tithe. And although no specific amount is commanded, Scripture makes plain our responsibility to give to the poor. When we look honestly at our finances, do we find that we are making excuses to ourselves about the amount we devote to good works? If so, then perhaps our god looks a bit more green and rectangular than we'd like to think.

One other area that makes a good honesty test is sex. If you have any doubt about what Scripture says about sex, Paul summarizes the position:

> Make no mistake: no fornicator or idolator, none who are guilty either of adultery or of homosexual perversion, no thieves or grabbers or drunkards or slanderers or swindlers, will possess the kingdom of

God.... "I am free to do anything," you may say. Yes but not everything is for my good. No doubt I am free to do anything, but I for one will not let anything make free with me. "Food is for the belly and the belly for food," you say. True, and one day God will put an end to both. But it is not true that the body is for lust; it is for the Lord— and the Lord for the body. God not only raised our Lord from the dead; he will also raise us by his power. Do you not know that your bodies are limbs and organs of Christ? Shall I then take from Christ his bodily parts and make them over to a harlot? Never! You surely know that anyone who links himself with a harlot becomes physically one with her (for Scripture says, "The pair shall become one flesh"); but he who links himself with Christ is one with him, spiritually. Shun fornication. Every other sin that a man can commit is outside his own body; but the fornicator sins against his own body. Do you not know that your body is a shrine of the indwelling Holy Spirit, and the Spirit is God's gift to you? You do not belong to yourselves; you were bought at a price. Then honor God in your body.
(1 Corinthians 6:9b-10, 12-20, NEB)

The guideline is clear: only heterosexual relationships within marriage are allowed. If this rule were universally followed, we would have no venereal disease, no AIDS, no murders committed because of infidelity, very little abortion, and far fewer split homes than we now have. A large percentage of our nation's welfare burden would be relieved, and the percentage of at-risk children in our educational system would be dramatically reduced. We know quite enough psychology to help us understand that these rules are for our own good, but our society almost never considers this corner of our psychological knowledge. Even without this knowledge, we Christians claim to have faith that the Bible represents a record of God's Word to humanity. It would seem reasonable to assume that, just perhaps, God knows even more than we do, and that therefore He might make some rules that are good for us even if we do not understand their purpose.

Now what have "modern" Christians done about God's sexual directions? First, many of us have decided that they are outdated. I know of no Christian who will argue that "Honor your father and your mother" or "Do not kill" are no longer God's commands. Yet "Do not commit adultery" is almost routinely ignored. Certainly Jesus defused the intention of the Jewish leaders to stone the woman taken in adultery. But his intention was not to justify her actions; rather, to contrast grace with judgmentalism. His words to the woman were "Go and sin no more" (John 8:11b).

> Elena grew up in a Christian home, went to a church-related college, and always considered her commitment to church a high priority. While in college, she became engaged to Al, and in her senior year, they slept together numerous times. Al and Elena married just after graduation, but split up after about five years. The years after her divorce saw Elena move more and more deeply into her church activities. She prepared for and passed two levels of ordination in her denomination, finally attaining the highest office short of priest. During this time, she met and began living with Jim, a successful attorney. She saw no conflict between her church position and her personal life.

Except for small details, the story of Elena, Al, and Jim is true. Unfortunately, it is also not uncommon. Even in the first-century church, similar problems existed. (See 1 Corinthians 5, for example.) How can people who say they are serious about their Christianity justify such a contradiction in their lives? I believe that these actions stem from devotion to too small a truth. The Declaration of Independence lists three inalienable rights: life, liberty, and the pursuit of happiness. There is no question that a Biblical basis can be found for asserting these rights in discussion of the relationship of government to the governed. But nowhere in Scripture is the pursuit of happiness accorded the stature of a fundamental need. Even in secular government, the right to pursue happiness is understood to have limits: when our happiness requires treading upon the rights of another, our rights to pursue that happiness end. For Christians, when our happiness requires breaking God's commandments, our rights to pursue that happiness end. Modern culture has elevated sexual pleasure to the level of a fundamental right. Scripture nowhere permits this view, although the Baal cults of the Canaanites encouraged it. Only by accepting this false view can we justify to ourselves the absurd notion that somehow the condom, the Pill, and abortion have eliminated the commandment against adultery. Like the god of casual sex, virtually all the false gods that we may worship partake of some small vestige of truth. But the Truth is that there is One God, and He is Agape-Love, not self-indulgence.

It would be very easy for us to continue, like good Pharisees, listing all the "Thou shalt not's" of Christian holiness. But rules are not what the Gospel is all about. Let's look at a prime method for growing in holiness: managing our stress.

The 1980's pop song "Don't Worry; Be Happy" became a standard joke because it trivializes the effect of emotions in our lives. But how do we stop worrying; how does one avoid rehearsing fear? The past few decades have seen much valuable research about the effect of stress on health. Seldom mentioned, though, is the fact that stress makes it harder for us not to worry. Hans Selye and others have devised stress tables that allow us to "score" our total stressors to see how much stress we're under. Later work has shown that some people can score well into the danger zone on stress tests and still manifest few symptoms of distress, while others who score lower may be incapacitated or even killed by the resulting distress. Studies of the lifestyles of the "stress survivors" indicate several behaviors common to these folk. First is a sense of purpose in life. As Christians, we have all been called to feed the hungry, help the poor, visit those who are sick or in prison, and witness to what we have experienced of Christ's work. We may become frustrated at times, but if we open our hearts to the needs of others, even to the virtual exclusion of our own needs, we will have purpose in living. If we instead concentrate on what we shall eat, what we shall wear, what we shall drive, and what our house and lawn look like, we will eventually find that it all is emptiness and chasing the wind. Dr. Norman Vincent Peale has stated that he had never known a person who suffered from clinical depression who was outward-focused. He believed that focusing on helping others was not only good religion, but also good medicine. I would add that an essential part of successfully focusing on others is to remember that "It is not the gardeners with their planting and watering who count, but God, who makes it grow" (1 Corinthians 3:7, NEB). Even trying to help others can become very depressing if we hold ourselves responsible for the results, since each person we try to help also has free will!

The second behavior common to stress survivors is play. Taking some time regularly at least two or three times a week, or preferably each day, to do something fun, is extremely important. The third anti-stress behavior is exercise. Certainly, these two can be effectively combined. A wise healer was once asked, "What is the best form of exercise for me?" He answered, "The one you'll actually do." Even competitive games are stress-relievers. Many physicians have stated that long, purposeful walks (not slow, meandering ambling) is the most healthful form of exercise. On days when weather or other impediments prevent our exercising, we can still play. Hobbies, board games, and even funny TV shows all work to relieve stress. Inspirational programs also help. In fact, in one experiment, watching a video of the life of Mother Teresa proved stress-relieving even for those who thought she was a fake and disapproved of her work. But tests have shown that shows involving conflict or violence, even verbal violence, actually increase stress. From a Christian point of view, if we take seriously what Paul said in Philippians 4:8— filling our thoughts with what is true, pure, noble, just, lovable, gracious, excellent, and admirable— we will probably find that most TV fare is not acceptable, even though some of it may strike us as funny. So using TV as play requires great caution, at least.

A fourth anti-stress behavior is appreciating beauty. Research has shown that "Type A" stressed-out people have usually lost their ability to really appreciate beauty in nature, music, art, or even other people. I have noticed this effect in myself from time to time. When I do, I must then choose to spend some time with music, which speaks most clearly to me, remembering what sections I especially enjoyed of a particular piece, concentrating on the *feeling* that the piece produced in me. By having chosen to spend the time, I avoid the frustration of feeling pulled away from something more urgent, and by concentrating on the feelings, I move my perception from the ever-whirring left brain which wants to list all the things I think I need to do, to my intuitive side, which can nurture me back to mental and emotional health if I allow it to.

Of course, there are many good books on stress management, and these can be a great help if you need to work on this area of your life. But let me mention just one more tactic before we move on: deep breaths. The Yogis and the Taoists discovered centuries ago that there is a physiological connection between deep, slow, "cleansing" breaths and relaxation. All deep-relaxation methods make use of this fact. You may remember that it was a part of our preparation for meditation. But deep breaths can also be used two or three at a time to abort stress whenever we feel it slipping up on us during our everyday activities. Many top managers, who must perform under enormous stress without losing their judgment, simply take two or three deep breaths and mentally focus on remembering a warm, love-filled, relaxing experience before making a critical judgment. When we do this, our heart rate and blood pressure drop measurably, hands and toes get warmer, and our minds are clearer.

Now the focus of this chapter is holiness. Haven't we wandered rather far from our topic? Not at all. Our western society has divided us into spiritual, mental, and physical parts. My truck has electrical, fuel, and mechanical systems. Its ignition and fuel systems are computer-controlled. But when a serious problem occurs in the fuel system, the computer may not be able to compensate for it, and performance suffers. Although separable into three parts, each of us is fundamentally one. Holiness is not a "religious" or "spiritual" thing; it is the way we live our lives each day. The quality of decisions we make— in other words, their consistency with our spiritual ideal— determines our holiness. Poorly managed stress damages our ability to make good decisions. It weakens us in the face of all kinds of temptations:

- It favors fear and weakens faith. When we are stressed out, we are more likely to worry about food and clothing and money. We place major importance on minor needs. We mentally turn small challenges into catastrophes.

Richard A. and Betty Jane Honeycutt 224

- It demands physical sensations for pleasure, since it blocks the avenues for appreciating purer pleasure. I think that there is no mystery in our society's fixation on sex and violence. Having adopted the god of materialism, we fall to stress when that god fails us. Then stress demands release through ever-stronger physical stimuli.
- It then takes advantage of our weakened, impure state to fill us with guilt and more fear that God cannot possibly forgive the condition we've fallen into.
- It deafens us to the still, small voice within.

If you recognize as much of yourself in this description as I do of myself, then we can agree that stress management is crucial to holiness.

The holy life comes down, then, to two things: holy intentions and the decisions to express them in holy actions. If we are to live as answers to Jesus's prayer in John 17, by being one with Him, we must confront and destroy our own personal gods that interfere with the worship of the One God. If we want to strengthen our prayer life, we must purify ourselves and live holy lives, not just to be good, but to be good for something!

> Here and now, dear friends, we are God's children; what we shall be has not yet been disclosed, but we know that when it is disclosed we shall be like him, because we shall see him as he is. Everyone who has this hope before him purifies himself, as Christ is pure.
> (1 John 1:2-3, NEB)

> Now that by obedience to the truth you have purified your souls until you feel sincere affection towards your brother Christians, love one another wholeheartedly with all your strength.
> (1 Peter 1:22)

To purify ourselves by obedience until we truly love our brothers takes work and sincere soul-searching. It is a lifetime job. But the benefits are eternal!

www.ingramcontent.com/pod-product-compliance
Lightning Source LLC
Chambersburg PA
CBHW060047100426
42742CB00014B/2726